Shaping a New Educational Landscape

Also available from Continuum

Regenerating Schools, Malcolm Groves

Leading the Leaders for the Future, Michael Bosher and Patrick Hazlewood

Personalizing Schools, Derek Wise

Personalizing Learning, John West-Burnham and Max Coates

The Constant Leader, Max Coates

Shaping a New Educational Landscape

Exploring possibilities for education in the 21st century

Edited by **Max Coates**

Foreword by **Dr Ann Holt OBE**
Future Schools

continuum

Continuum International Publishing Group

The Tower Building
11 York Road
London SE1 7NX

80 Maiden Lane
Suite 704
New York NY 10038

www.continuumbooks.com

© Max Coates and contributors 2010

British Library Cataloguing-in-Publication Data
A catalogue record for this book is available from the British Library.

ISBN: 9780826432582 (paperback)

Library of Congress Cataloging-in-Publication Data
Coates, Max.
 Shaping a new educational landscape : creating a new context for
learning / Max Coates.
     p. cm.
 ISBN 978-0-8264-3258-2 (pbk.)
1. Educational change. 2. Education—Forcasting. 3. School
improvement programs. I. Title.

 LB41.5.C63 2010
 370.1—dc22

                                           2009038028

Typeset by Ben Cracknell Studios
Printed and bound in Great Britain by MPG Book Group Ltd

Contents

About the authors

Professor Paul Clarke

Paul is currently completing a new book on the theme of creating sustainable communities. This work has been undertaken online in the form of a blog (www.sustainableretreat. blogspot.com) and focuses on the principles, design, development and practice of sustainable community. He is a co-director of the Incredible Edible programme and works alongside gardeners, doctors, unemployed people, students, teachers, shopkeepers, business people, prisons, you name it, to generate practical solutions to complex challenges of living, learning, dreaming and loving life.

Paul has worked as a teacher, teacher adviser and university lecturer in the education field since the mid 1980s. He is currently the director and co-founder of IQEST – a social enterprise organization that is engaged in research and development projects in the UK and overseas, and is attempting to instil a human-scale response to change in public sector reform.

Alongside this work in IQEST, he is a lead consultant in the IQEA – the Improving the Quality of Education for All programme – and he regularly works with schools and networks of schools around the world on improvement programmes. Much of this work forms the basis of his writing and commentary in books and journals.

Paul is Professor of Sustainable Education at St Mary's University College, London. His interests in professional learning are focused on how the workplace organizes its relationships. His interest is not on the tasks and functions, and hierarchies that are created, but rather he is looking at the patterns of relationships, how we learn to tolerate irregularities and use them productively and how we support people as they try to form lasting and valued partnerships which solve problems.

Max Coates

Max Coates was a secondary head for 12 years. He is a senior post-graduate lecturer in leadership at St Mary's University College. He has also been Team Programme Manager for the London Centre for Leadership in Learning. Over the last few years he has worked extensively in the area of leadership, emotional intelligence and mentoring and coaching both in the UK and abroad. Of note has been a range of work carried out with local authorities. He is also a lead consultant for the Network of Black Professionals and is the Educational Design Consultant for Chapel Street. A significant recent development has been the use of a motivational diagnostic to understand and extend teams and also the development of programmes and consultancy around integrated children's services. He is currently undertaking work for The Leadership Development for Schools (Republic of Ireland). Published works include books on personalizing learning, and citizenship and a recent book, *The Constant Leader*, which explores surviving and thriving in leadership and management. He is married with three allegedly grown up sons and lives in Dorset!

Steve Coates

My name is Steve Coates, 20, and I am currently studying Interactive Media Production at Bournemouth University. I also am a keen performance musician. I have a growing local reputation as a guitarist and singer and also love listening to a wide variety of music. I have edited a number of distance-learning materials which have been used in a wide range of schools and I also produce and maintain websites for a number of businesses and individuals.

Dame Pat Collarbone

Dame Pat Collarbone taught for 28 years in inner London and was a very successful headteacher of a secondary school in Hackney. In 1997 she founded the London Leadership Centre at the Institute of Education, University of London. She was the Executive Director of the National Remodelling Team during its existence and has been a Director of the National College for School Leadership (NCSL) and an Executive Director of the Training and Development Agency for Schools (TDA). In 2008 she co-authored a book on systems leadership and has recently published a book on remodelling. She now runs Education Change Associates Ltd and is a Director of Creating Tomorrow Ltd. She is a visiting professor at the University of Christchurch Canterbury and a visiting fellow at the Institute of Education. She was made a Dame in 1997 for services to education.

Richard Crabtree

Richard Crabtree has a BA(Hons) in Economics and a MSc in International Business Economics from UWE, Bristol. Post graduation he has spent 14 years in banking, global communications and IT services.

Dr John Eaton

Dr John Eaton has practised as a registered psychotherapist since 1989 in both private practice and for the UK National Health Service.

He is also the founder of Reverse Therapy – an educational process closely linked to emotional intelligence training – which relieves the symptoms of stress-related illnesses.

John fears that education was wasted on him but that has not stopped him from teaching numerous courses, from Psychology at A Level to Psychotherapy at Masters Level. John graduated with a doctorate from Lancaster University Department of Psychology in 1998 and is a member of the British Psychological Society.

He has written, or co-written, five books: *Coaching Successfully* (1999), *Influencing People* (2000), *Communicating with Emotional Intelligence* (2001), *Reverse Therapy* (2005), *Reverse Therapy for Health* (2007), and numerous articles on psychology and psychotherapy.

Professor Alma Harris

Alma Harris is Pro-Director (Leadership) at the Institute of Education, London and Chair in Educational Leadership at the London Centre for Leadership in Learning. Her research work focuses on organizational change and development. She is internationally known for her work on school improvement, focusing particularly on improving schools in challenging circumstances.

She is currently co-directing a large scale DCSF project on 'Leadership and Learning Outcomes', an ESRC study on 'Multi-agency Leadership' and is currently co-directing a project focused on high performing organizations in the sectors of education, business, health and sport.

Her most recent work has focused on distributed leadership and 'Distributed School Leadership: Developing Tomorrow's Leaders'.

Her website can be located at http://www.almaharris.co.uk.

Professor David Hopkins

David Hopkins is Professor Emeritus at the Institute of Education, University of London where, until recently, he held the inaugural HSBC iNet Chair in International Leadership. He is a Trustee of Outward Bound, holds visiting professorships at the Catholic University of Santiago, the Chinese University of Hong Kong and the Universities of Edinburgh, Melbourne and Wales and consults internationally on school reform. Between 2002 and 2005 he served three Secretaries of State as the Chief Adviser on School Standards at the Department for Education and Skills.

Previously, he was Chair of the Leicester City Partnership Board and Dean of the Faculty of Education at the University of Nottingham. Before that again he was a tutor at the University of Cambridge Institute of Education, a secondary school teacher and Outward Bound instructor. David is also an International Mountain Guide who still climbs regularly in the Alps and Himalayas. The Open University Press published his most recent books, *Every School a Great School* and *System Leadership in Practice*.

Caitlin Lord

My name is Caitlin Grace Lord. I have just turned 12 and I am currently in Year 7 at St Michael's Middle School in Wimborne.

I love my family and am madly in love with my cat Billy and my new kitten Ollie. My favourite music groups are The Fray, The Script and Ben Folds 5. I also enjoy Taylor Swift, Colbie Caillat, Jack Johnson and Jason Mraz. I really enjoy outdoor activities such as high ropes, caving, kayaking, etc. I am also a bookworm. I love hanging out with my friends.

Russell Rook

Following 18 years working in the voluntary and faith-based sectors Russell is now the Chief Executive of Chapel Street, a social enterprise working to deliver alternative education and healthcare in the UK's most deprived communities. Formerly he worked with The Salvation Army where he headed up the ALOVE initiative delivering services to young people and young adults in the UK and Ireland and was one of the founders of YOUTHWORK – the partnership. Russell's theological work addresses the role of culture in human belief and behaviour. He teaches in a wide array of settings and is at present working on a new project focusing on the subject of ethics.

Jan-Paul van Staalduinen

Jan-Paul van Staalduinen is a PhD researcher in the Systems Engineering Group of the Faculty of Technology, Policy and Management of Delft University of Technology. His research interests are education, social software and serious games. His PhD thesis focuses on the integration of educational theory and game design methods. In 2004 he got his Masters in Systems Engineering and Policy Analysis at the TU Delft, with a thesis on scenarios for education support infrastructures.

After graduating he worked as an e-learning consultant for the TU Delft. After that he worked at Unisys Netherlands, as a process analyst and trainer. From 2006 to 2008 he worked for the consultancy firm Verdonck, Klooster & Associates, where he helped governmental bodies with projects on ICT policy and strategy, information management and quality management. He has been a full-time PhD researcher since July 2008. In his spare time he teaches adults presentation and debating skills for an educational foundation.

Will Thomas

Will wrote *Coaching Solutions*, the first book of its kind to take coaching approaches from the business sector and apply them directly to education. He has a 20-year history of research in coaching and creativity and is renowned for his highly relevant training, coaching and prolific writing. A former Marks and Spencer manager and School Curriculum Leader, he now runs Vision for Learning, providing inspirational training and coaching support. In 2007 he founded The Institute of Educational Coaching (IEC), dedicated to raising awareness of coaching in education. He is part of the creative school development team 'Thank Goodness It's Monday' which supports organizations to grow authentic, values-driven approaches to leadership. Will has supported thousands of educationalists to develop coaching skills and professional reflection in the UK and in British and American schools abroad. In his spare time he is a passionate advocate of The Duke of Edinburgh's Award and principal advisor to The Manisha Child Welfare Fund, Nepal, an education charity. He combines fundraising for the charity with what he describes as 'a limited talent, but limitless enthusiasm, for triathlon'. Will believes passionately that self-awareness is the key to acting responsibly. Will may be contacted through his website www.visionforlearning.co.uk.

Professor Wim Veen

Wim Veen (1946) is professor of Education and Technology at Delft University of Technology. He has been involved in institutional strategies for educational innovations at his university. He researches the development of new concepts and models for ICT-enabled learning in both the private and public sector. He introduced the concept of Homo Zappiens, a generation of learners with new learning strategies demanding flexible and participative education. Together with a multi-disciplinary team of researchers he contributes to e-learning developments in organizations where new learning cultures are emerging for a knowledge intensive and creative economy.

Key ideas in his view are:

- Game developers are excellent educationalists
- Learning and working are intimate lovers
- Knowledge is communication about meaning

Dr Raphael Wilkins

Raphael Wilkins is Pro Director (London), and Director of Consultancy, LCLL, in the Institute of Education, University of London. He is also Dean and Vice-President of the College of Teachers. Before joining the Institute in 2006, his career included teaching; education officer roles in four local authorities including over 12 years in Chief Officer-level posts; national roles with parliament and the local authority associations; six years of freelance senior-level consultancy, research and writing; and attachments to a number of universities. Raphael has published over 50 articles and research reports, has led many workshops on leadership issues, and has presented papers or keynotes at education conferences in Britain, Denmark, The Netherlands, Canada, USA, India and China.

Chris Wright

Chris Wright MA, FRSA, Director of Education for the Woodard Corporation. Previously a headteacher in both the maintained and independent sector as well as director of an international school, Chris has been a lecturer in education at King's College, London and a facilitator for the National College of School Leadership. He is the author of 25 books on education, primarily in the field of religious education.

Professor John West-Burnham

John West-Burnham is a writer, teacher and consultant in education leadership with a particular interest in leadership learning and development and learning in schools and communities. He has been a school teacher, teacher trainer, education officer and has held posts in five universities. He is Professor of Educational Leadership at St Mary's University College, Twickenham. John is the author or editor of 23 books and he has worked in 24 countries.

Dr Chris Yapp

Chris, until recently, has been an Executive Technology Strategy Consultant with Capgemini UK. He has been in the IT industry since 1980, most recently at Microsoft. He has worked extensively across the public sector in local government, education, health and creative industries. Chris's interests lie in scenario planning, futurology and the strategic and management implications of ICTs. He has edited and contributed to a number of books, most recently *Personalization of Learning in the 21st Century*. He is an Associate of the Think Tank DEMOS. He is a Fellow of both the RSA and the BCS.

He is a Patron of NACE and a Trustee of World e-citizens. He is a member of the Information Society Panel of UNESCO UK. He is a member of the BERR Industry forum for the Communications and Content Industries.

Chris holds a MA (Oxon) and an honorary DTech from Glasgow Caledonian.

Preface

Max Coates, December 2009

Against the backdrop of a rapidly changing world, formal schooling is frequently following rather than leading. The impression is often given by central government that the education system serves as a 'thermostat', restoring society's settings in areas such as productivity, citizenship, health, behaviour and sexual mores, to name but a few.

The perception of writers and thinkers such as the founder of Visa, Dee Hock, and the former Czech President, Václav Havel, is that we are at a point of transition comparable with the move from the medieval period to the enlightenment, a time when there is little predictability but everything to play for. Schools are potentially at the pinnacle of their development in relationship to this passing epoch but have diminishing relevance in an unfolding age, which has still to be defined.

Some years ago in a woodworking magazine there was an article on how to make a rocking horse. The instructions were terse; take a large block of wood and cut away everything that does not look like a horse. In a sense there is a parallel with the way in which our society is seeking to understand itself, not in terms of what it is, but rather in terms of what it is not. The main descriptors usually have the word 'post' in them. So society is described as being post-industrial, post-modern, post-Christian or post-enlightenment.

Shaping a New Educational Landscape is a collection of chapters that explore possibilities rather than simply reiterating the present as a signpost to future formation. The writers are all highly respected. The importance of their contributions is not in being able to make accurate predictions about the future but rather through their writings to unsettle current thinking and assumptions and to stimulate debate about what might be.

Twenty-two years of the Educational Reform Act (1988) has clarified an existing educational process, reformatted the financial management of schools and resuscitated the inspection system. It has arguably not laid the foundations of a world-class, future responsive educational system.

The recently published McKinsey Report (2007) summarizes evidence that demonstrates that increase in expenditure has not produced commensurate outcomes in terms of student/pupil performance. Concurrently the emergence of personalization on the educational agenda has, in the main, produced limited innovative practice and all too often it has been diluted to a focus on ICT and a distorted minimalist understanding of learning styles.

This book is a self-conscious enterprise to rattle the bars of the educational cage. It is about stimulating the generation of an educational process that will sponsor new economic paradigms and create a bold participative society on the new global stage. Education must be fit for purpose. The current hiatus lies with the uncertainties around the definition of that purpose. Without a profound review there is a danger that our education system will remain well placed if the 1950s should ever come round again.

The book is divided into three sections:

1   The Future is Now
2   The Evolving School
3   The Changing Classroom

I would like to formally express my thanks to the contributors. Some are personal friends, some I have not even met, but all are fellow travellers with a passion to see young people facing the future equipped and empowered by hope and with a vision of possibilities of what might be. In particular, I would like to express my thanks to the staff at Continuum Press for allowing me to birth this idea. Thanks are due to my long-suffering family, especially my wife, Sally, who has engaged with the project by proxy.

The challenges facing UK schools are not parochial but are contiguous with those charged with the provision of education in every continent. As I visit different countries I have seen learning taking place in sophisticated buildings equipped with complex ICT systems and elsewhere seen schools of 10,000 working in two daily shifts and receiving instruction in lots of 100. As I am writing, UK education budgets are being pruned as a result of the recession. Some of the schools I visit would not have anything to prune and yet there is the same need to harness young minds to engineer the future of our planet. The educational provision for these young people is modest but they too are part of that global enterprise called education. The authors of this book readily and enthusiastically agreed to donate their royalties to Juba Secondary School in the Sudan. This has allowed us to express, in a modest way, a solidarity with colleagues who share that same hope for coming generations and yet who lack the rudimentary tools of their craft. We hope in some small way that we can gives their energies and professional courage added impetus. The Sudan has been devastated by war – just maybe we can contribute to restoration through education.

The book is dedicated to Caity and Steve. It is their generation that must face and forge the future of our world.

Foreword

Canon Dr Ann Holt, OBE

Default positions die very hard especially when they are the product of vested interests. That we live in a rapidly changing world where the landscape really is changing, literally, (it is reported that the west coast of South Island, New Zealand is 12 inches closer to Australia as a result of recent volcanic activity) is a truism but what is astonishing is the unwillingness of institutions, be they those of government, the educational establishment or parents, genuinely to embrace change as opposed to talking about it, especially when they may need to give up cherished shibboleths or just a child-minding service. Wilkins (page 91) states 'while governments use the language of innovation and transformation, they do not in practice stray far from tried and tested approaches to educational provision'. My experience exactly and an argument for restricting that for which government is responsible and cannot deliver any way, yet for which they will be blamed if it goes wrong because they have set themselves up to be so. Meanwhile the rest of us abdicate our responsibilities. Big state can be very seductive all round.

At the time of writing we are in the middle of a financial crisis which has called into question the whole economic basis upon which our society is predicated and to which our education has been subservient since the Industrial Revolution. And yet there is a real possibility that in the medium term nothing will really change if we manage to escape, for a while, the worst exigencies of the near collapse of capitalism as we know it. Will we, as Thomas puts it (page 110), 'ask questions of our . . . growth-based presuppositions'?

If we fail to read the signs of what is happening we shall fail to make the changes needed in our globalized, and at the same time localized, society in general and those changes in education in particular, some of which are heralded in this book. At a time when the rhetoric is that of innovation, entrepreneurialism, personalized learning, interdependence, community . . . we are in the process creating institutionalized human beings (homo institutionaligens), some of whom enter their first institution, a nursery, at two and end their days aged 92 in a nursing home, having passed through a variety of institutions, academic, training and workplace, in between. But still we wonder why we lack the imagination to enjoy and respond to a wonderfully complex world. The situation is not helped by the fact that we still applaud, despite the alternative rhetoric, those institutions such as our public schools, Russell Group universities, the professions of law and medicine, as the epitome of success and they, in turn, are among the most critical of any moves to changing what they perceive to be the 'gold standard' even though for the majority it is not fit for purpose. Of course, as Wright reminds us, behind the conservative exterior, there is often a high degree of experimentation going on which no one queries because of the high level of ostensible success and the espousal of enduring and traditional values. This confirms the thesis that for the time being only those enjoying success on current terms will be allowed the 'luxury' of innovation.

Recent articles in the media have lambasted the failure to open up medicine and the law to a wider social group but no comment was made about the greater diversity of equally lucrative and desirable professions into which far greater numbers than ever of university graduates go in the post-modern society. It seems that we still collude with one another to create a narrow hierarchy of socially acceptable professions. In the words of Paul Clarke (page 80), 'community and school are stuck in a perpetual cycle of dependency of the worst possible kind'.

This is where we must now be careful, however, because another powerful obstacle to change has been the educational establishment's own insistence on the rhetoric of autonomy. In the seventeenth century the poet and philosopher, John Donne, reminded us that no human being is an island. Living is normally an interdependent activity. Although the trend towards personalized learning is a welcome antidote to the battery farming models of pedagogy redolent of the nineteenth century, rather than the twenty-first, it must never become a recipe for individualism and a failure to prepare learners to live in community.

The so-called 'Red Tory', Philip Blonde, now working at Demos, speaks of the urgent need to fill the gap between big state which has been the stance of serial governments since the 1980s and the disconnected, autonomous individual. In short part of the moral purpose of education must be to help rebuild the notions of society and community in the twenty-first century.

It is in the writings of the great social prophet, Neil Postman, particularly in his book *The End of Education*, that we find him saying that to be effective education needs a big story, a narrative, as Hopkins puts it, or in Michael Fullan's terminology, a moral purpose, a compelling vision. Otherwise we are in danger of setting in train a pandemic of 'information aids' potentially as dangerous as the biological variety. We have already experienced in acts of terrorism the outcomes of irresponsibly knowing how to do something coupled with an immoral purpose. In the Jewish tradition from which Postman came to know is to become responsible. 'Homo Zappiens' needs the gift of discernment more than ever before. Education for character is vital. Somewhat unwisely, I have been heard to say that I would go to the stake, not for the Education Reform Act of 1988 *per se* but for the rubric that cites the importance of the role of schools in the spiritual, moral, social and cultural development of pupils as well as the cognitive If the systemic changes described in these essays are to become more truly transformational rather than mere tinkering with the system, then they have to be fuelled by a far bigger ambition for each learner than five A–C grades at GCSE. Child well-being has to be defined in more than economic terms. The Every Child Matters agenda is just too reductionist to inspire the change that our world demands. To borrow the words of Russell Rook, we need a 'thicker' vision. An ecology of the classroom in which all are welcomed, adult and young person, and where profound respect for the 'other' is fostered which begins to form the basis of a genuine community of education way beyond the provision of extended services to keep children off the streets until their exhausted parents get home.

I have spent a good part of my working life in education, latterly supporting and developing school governors, who are the bridge at the local leadership level between the school as an organization and the wider community in which it functions. We may have given them too many tasks to perform but we have seriously underestimated their performance potential by failing to engage them in the debates that this book ought to stimulate and then using them to mobilize parents and the wider community to help change the normative and environmental factors in the educational landscape into the ones that we now urgently need to develop and to which the institutions need to adapt.

So to be followers of tradition, government policy, the latest fashion . . . or leaders of social transformation? That is the question for those involved in education everywhere. There are innumerable testimonies of where education has changed individual lives worldwide. I am one of them. But we need to change the world, not just individuals. The poverty of an econometrically driven world view needs to be exposed in favour of one that develops a discerning imagination. Schooling cannot do it on its own but it has to be in the vanguard of change. Ideas really do have legs. It is my hope that many of the ideas of the passionate people who have contributed to this book will indeed walk their way deeply into our education system. If they do, we stand a chance locally of developing something world class for our own children and contributing to the global common good. Education, education, education could then have some real substance.

Part 1
THE FUTURE IS NOW

1 Future tense

Max Coates

When shall we three meet again?
In thunder, lightning, or in rain?

Macbeth Act 1 Scene 1

The prediction of the future has fascinated people through the ages. The lines quoted above are from a play where much of the appeal is the interplay of real-time events against the backdrop of supernatural revelation. In actuality, the old crones were not that great at soothsaying if they actually had to discuss when they were going to hold their next meeting.

The past is open to interpretation, the present to perception and the future is inevitably about speculation. The projections offered are seldom objective and often reflect either a dystopian or utopian perspective rooted either in the social climate of the time or even in the personal circumstances of the writer. H. G. Wells wrote the utopian novel *Men Like Gods* derived from the optimism of modernity. George Orwell's stance was clearly dystopian in *1984*, a 'house of horrors' where a regime was presented that would go to any lengths to own and possess history, to rewrite and reconstruct it, and to inculcate it by means of coercion. While these are fictional works they have often become reference points in our thinking and frequently serve to define current experience. Fictional ideas often take root in forming our world view. Boudrillard (1985), dubbed the prophet of post-modernity, wrote a series of essays called *Simulacra and Simulation* of which the leatherbound edition famously briefly appears in the opening scenes of *The Matrix*. These examine the power of representations in an image-fixated post-modern world.

> Audiences are so saturated in representations that these now precede perceptions of the actual, subtly changing them in the process. (page 22)

For many, their first brush with a futurologist (though the term futurist is now preferred, to distance their work from activities such as astrology) was Alvin Toffler. In 1970 he wrote *Future Shock*, which identified the impact of the changes derived from burgeoning knowledge and high-speed connectivity between people and organizations. It was argued that human beings would buckle under the impact of the knowledge explosion. *Future*

Shock sold over six million copies; intriguingly it was an extension of an article originally written for *Playboy* magazine.

Many futurists shock the reader with a torrent of current statistics, which often use numbers with more zeros on the end than our national debt. The following is from a recent book by Alvin and Heidi Toffler (2006):

> In 2002 the Japanese built a computer called the Earth Simulator designed to help forecast global climate changes. It performed 40,000 billion calculations per second – faster than its seven closest rivals combined. By 2005, IBM had reclaimed the lead with a supercomputer twice as fast, and scientists predict that computers may reach petaflop speeds – a thousand trillion mathematical operations a second – by the end of the decade.
>
> Meanwhile, the number of Internet users worldwide is estimated at between 700,000,000 and 900,000,000. (page 7)

Such astonishing facts actually do little to validate the authors' subsequent projections.

The case for future's thinking is further undermined by some notable failures. Consider the following spectacularly misguided predictions:

- 'All the calculations that would ever be needed in this country could be done on the three digital computers, which were then being built – one in Cambridge, one in Teddington, and one in Manchester. No one else would ever need machines of their own, or would be able to afford to buy them.' Professor Douglas Hartree, 1951.
- We don't like their sound, and guitar music is on the way out.' Decca Recording Co. rejecting the Beatles, 1962.

Despite the humour derived from such prophetic banana skins, future's thinking is not merely desirable but arguably essential in the leading and shaping the provision of education. Without such thinking there are at least four undesirable outcomes:

1. *Clinging to the past*: simply going back to an imagined golden age is unlikely to do the job – schools have to change to meet the challenges of a different world, and provide an education that is fit for purpose – the question is, how?
2. *Buying the official line:* faced with the sheer uncertainty of the future, it is all too easy to retreat into a reliance on policy documents and other people's visions, but these seldom provide a reliable guide.
3. *Defeatism:* faced with the uncertainty of the future, some people simply give up trying to influence it and decide to let things take their course.
4. *Placing to greater an emphasis on managerialism:* the major preoccupation becomes the matching of finite resources to perceived problems.

Michael Fullan (1998) concluded that the pressure of the immediate induces school leaders to be vulnerable to quick-fix solutions and fosters a culture of dependency on external agencies.

> Realizing that there is no answer, that we will never arrive in any formal sense, can be quite liberating. Instead of hoping that the latest technique will at last provide the answer, we approach the situation differently. Leaders for change get involved as learners in real reform situations. They craft their own theories of change, consistently testing them against new situations. They become critical consumers of management theories, able to sort out promising ideas from empty ones. They become less vulnerable to and less dependent on external answers. They stop looking for solutions in the wrong places. (page 2)

As the poet Antonio Machado wrote, 'Life is a path you beat while you walk it'.

With Fullan's caveat fully in mind there are still trustworthy travelling companions to scan the horizon with us. Consider the reflections of the then Czech President, Václav Havel in his speech delivered in Philadelphia on 4 July 1994:

> I think there are good reasons for suggesting that the modern age has ended. Today, many things indicate that we are going through a transitional period, when it seems that something is on the way out and something else is painfully being born. It is as if something were crumbling, decaying, and exhausting itself – while something else, still indistinct, were rising from the rubble.

Havel's words resonate strongly with those of Dee Hock, the founder and ex-CEO of Visa:

> We are at that very point in time when a four-hundred-year-old age is rattling in its deathbed and another is struggling to be born. A shifting of culture, science, society and institutions enormously greater and swifter than the world has ever experienced. Ahead, lies the possibility of regeneration of individuality, liberty, community and ethics such as the world has never known, and a harmony with nature, with one another and with the divine intelligence such as the world has never seen. It is the path to a livable future in the centuries ahead, as society evolves into ever-increasing diversity and complexity. (Hock, 2005: page 10)

The 400-year-old break-point referred to is the transition from the medieval period to the enlightenment. The former was a period where the prevailing world view, whether expressed in terms of cosmology or social organization, was one of finite boundaries perceived as being imposed by a divine purpose. The enlightenment, on the other hand, assumed a paradigm of human optimism with unfettered learning establishing truth, understanding and the solution to human problems. This transitional point was not clearly defined. The reality was messy and most present would have been unaware that they were at a defining point.

Hock's argument is that we are at another fork in the road of human history, though it is not the intention of this book to explore this change in detail. The following are offered as indicators and not definitions of this transition:

- The development of communications both in terms of speed and personal access.
- Globalization with its 24/7 engagement and wakefulness.
- A lack of confidence in a mechanistic worldview as the indeterminacy of post-Einsteinium theories of relativity has become assimilated into popular thinking (just think of *Dr Who*). The sub-plot is that even science is not as straightforward as we thought it was and is definitely not as reliable!
- Institutional authority is being freely challenged whether political, in our schools or at our health centres and hospitals.
- The ownership of knowledge and learning has broken through established protocols and elites.

The previous quotation by Dee Hock is optimistic but hopes for a positive outcome are not inevitable and some three years before the 'credit crunch' he offered this alternative, bleaker possibility:

> Unfortunately, ahead lies equal possibility of massive institutional failure, enormous social carnage and regression to that ultimate manifestation of Newtonian, mechanistic concepts of organization, dictatorship, which, in turn, would have to collapse with even more carnage before new concepts of organization could emerge. (Hock, 2005: page 11)

Without wishing to labour the point our world has changed and has done so at an exponential rate. For example, a moment's reflection on the emergence of China as the workshop of the world has huge implications for our society, economy and our schools especially in the area of curriculum design and development. Fifty years ago 80 per cent of the population made or moved something. Now it is less than 10 per cent with most of the workforce currently making their jobs up as they go along. Generating workers for the leisure and tourism industry can only soak up so many of the industrially dispossessed.

Much of our current planning in education, however, still seems to assume that the future will be a modified version of the past. Such a view is a triumph of optimism over reality.

Engaging with future's thinking

A fire drill will never correspond exactly with the actual emergency but it provides a way of rehearsing a response and establishing contingency planning. In a similar way 'future's thinking' encourages an organization, or indeed a system, to rehearse its response to potential future developments.

Perhaps of even greater significance is that journey forward changes. The established route of the train journey gives way to the flexibility of the car. Future's thinking engages individuals and teams with innovation and there is a move from replication to regeneration, from predictability to possibility.

Consider by way of example the development of the curriculum. The starting point remains largely subject-centred. Even the recent review of the primary curriculum by Sir Jim Rose was more about rebalancing skills and knowledge and single subjects and cross-curricular studies. Mike Baker commenting for the BBC suggested that:

> But it seems the national curriculum continues to be the repository of a very wide range of subjects and of every worthwhile activity from cookery to citizenship.
>
> It seems the politicians and the experts are not ready to set a very simple primary national curriculum, with a compulsory core of little more than maths and English, while leaving the rest to teachers' discretion. (2009)

Supposing curriculum reform started with a blank sheet of paper and consideration was given to the fact that knowledge is not self-evidently contained in silos. Additionally if the design recognized the short shelf-life of knowledge in a twenty-first century world and where feast has replaced famine. The discoveries in the neurosciences in the last ten years, while still not coherent, still demand a tectonic shift from teaching to learning. Consider the impact of a primary curriculum based on the Reggio Emilia Approach with its requirement that children must have some control over the direction of their learning. Perhaps we would not have started from here. Future's thinking, while not committed to destroying what is, does open the eyes to what might be.

Currently some of the most useful developments in future's thinking have come from the work by the think tank Demos. Their approach is to generate a range of scenarios. Crucial is that these are not merely 'back of an envelope' thinking. In formulating the scenarios great care is taken to generate from a stance of rigorous thinking grounded in a careful analysis of the current situation. They advocate the use of PESTEL; this seems to capture most dimensions:

- **P**olitical – e.g., likely election results, political participation, policy trends
- **E**conomic – e.g., likely economic growth, poverty rates, changes in national and international markets
- **S**ocial – e.g., levels of individualism
- **T**echnological – e.g., developments in computing, biotechnology
- **E**nvironmental – e.g., impact of climate change
- **L**egal – e.g., likely changes in law

This process is then often augmented by brainstorming to generate the best scenarios that are possible. The design of the scenarios is then further refined by exploring 'important' and 'uncertain' factors. These Demos understand as:

- Trends that are important and unpredictable. Often known as 'critical uncertainties', these trends are the most important to consider.
- Trends that are important but predictable – factors like demography, and climate change. These are things we know will happen in the future.
- Trends that are unimportant, and therefore shouldn't be a priority for thinking about the future.

Overall some six scenarios are generated and explored and possibilities for planning and action are investigated. In the process it develops leadership capacity and capability such that the situations that eventually take place will be met with a robust response.

It is worth reflecting on the fact that, at the time of writing, no staff in our schools under the age of 42 have worked in a school environment not prescribed by the 1988 Education Reform Act. It would be cynical to describe the process of the last 20 years as 'teaching by numbers'. However it has certainly not generated a climate which has been fertile to innovative thinking.

Ten year ago Brent Davies and Linda Ellison (1999) were advocating that schools should have a three-stage model for planning based on:

- Development and operational planning for 1–3 years
- Strategic intent and strategic planning for 3–5 years
- Future's thinking based around looking forward 5–15 years (page 27)

Their research with 40 schools showed that:

- All 40 had a plan for 1–3 years
- Five had a formal planning process for 3–5 years
- Seven had done some future's thinking (page 38)

It is not clear whether the situation has significantly changed, however cursory investigation suggests that future's thinking remains separated from a secure methodology. Fresh thinking in a stable setting is merely invention; such thinking in a rapidly changing context is innovation. Tom Bentley, the then Director of Demos, commented:

> We need to avoid a trap. We need to ask what is the most appropriate kind of education for young people. Then how schools can best act as providers and brokers in creating learning opportunities. The challenge for school leaders is to create the space for new possibilities. (2005)

Future's thinking is an imperative but must be supported by engaging with reliable resources and appropriate methodologies.

Interleaf
How I see the future

Caitlin Lord, age 12

My opinion on the future may not be accurate; it is just my point of view. One of the main things that I think will affect our world the most is that we will become much more reliant on technology. We will develop to the point that I think we will rely entirely on technology, for example for shopping, schooling and communicating. I think a lot of sensitive information will be stored about each member of society on government computers. Technology is very useful and is helpful with a lot of things, but it may cause a risk of becoming obese. If we carry on developing new systems that don't require much physical activity, at the rate we're going now, there is every chance of this. Therefore the effect of technology on our lives definitely will be massive but I can't say whether it will be altogether positive.

I think that in the future we will have schooling on computers at home and there will be a virtual teacher, who will almost be holographic. As a possible result of this, children may become anti-social.

For transport, I think we will develop hover cars for people to get around faster, which will be run on some eco-friendly energy. Also, I think our natural resources such as crude oil will run out, but I think we will find another source of energy, which possibly could be from tidal and wind power. We definitely will have polluted the earth a lot and will find the air hard to breathe in.

I reckon there will be huge medical breakthroughs, for example a more effective cure for cancer and the growth of organs for transplanting.

Religion, I think, will be a cause of war between people, but I believe there will be a growth in religion as people look to find some hope.

What I think I will be like in the future is: I think I would be a bit lazy, considering all the things we now do may be replaced by a computer or robot, but I hope I'm not like that. From what I think about the future you can sense that I'm not sure if planet earth will be a positive place to live in, but let's wait and see.

That is the future through my eyes.

2 The shape of the future

Chris Yapp

There is an eternal tension at the heart of education. On the one hand we see education as a process of transferring the best of our knowledge, experience, culture and values from one generation to another. At the same time, we seek to prepare one generation for a future different from the present reality for us as adults.

I argue that it is a conceit of each generation to believe that its challenges are unique. Most famously we can find quotes back to Roman times that show adults worrying about feral, unkempt and uncaring youth. *Plus ça change*?

It is frequently argued that we are going through a period of rapid and widespread change. Whether the challenge is technological change, globalization or climate change from our vantage point many commentators feel that our ability to understand the future is extremely challenged.

Now of course, we can find quotes that show that we have never been very good at seeing into the future. Famous examples include 'I can see a market for maybe five computers' or 'Cinema is an invention of no consequence'.

Most recently, Nasim Nicholas Taleb in his book *The Black Swan* has lobbed an intellectual hand grenade at those who have built, and believed in, quantitative models of the future.

I remember many years ago a funny parody which argued that 'we ran an empire when the core of our education was Dickens, Latin and spin bowling. That seemed good enough'.

So, do we give up on preparing future minds or is the best we can do to transmit from one generation to the next?

My starting point is to ask what we can know of the future from our historical views of the future. From that I believe that we can create a framework to discuss the future. This includes the necessary humility to know how little we might understand of the future.

My aim is to create a working hypothesis about the future which informs, rather than determines, our efforts to prepare a rising generation through learning to survive and thrive whatever future unravels.

Let us consider some observations that I believe help us to see what is possible.

1 The human condition changes slowly

While society changes, technology changes and our knowledge of the world changes, sometimes very rapidly, we evolve slowly as a species. Of course, there are periods for particular groups where war, genocide or epidemic can have a significant impact. This is why my second observation lies at the core of my argument.

2 Stories have the power to explore and explain

All human societies have their stories, fables, myths and legends. It is quite remarkable how Aesop's Fables can still be understood today. I remember a few years ago being at a performance of *King Lear* in Croatia. I spoke to people who were amazed at how Shakespeare spoke to the culture and history of Croatia. I can remember a hot, sunny day at Haworth in Yorkshire and watching a bus full of Japanese tourists, many of whom were carrying Brontë books. The Leonardo de Caprio film *Romeo and Juliet* set in modern California again illustrates the capacity of stories to transcend time, cultural boundaries and geography.

Over the last 50 years, the development of scenario planning has been one of the key features of 'futurology'. Scenarios are not predictions, but stories about the future which organizations use to test their plans, to uncover implicit assumptions and to communicate visions of the future. Of course, with the rich media we now enjoy, stories can be in books, games, TV, film, animation and many forms yet to be developed, no doubt.

3 Our actions, individually and collectively can make a difference

One aspect of scenario planning is that rather than create a single vision of the future, it creates a set of scenarios which are plausible but different in character to each other. The value of scenarios often lies in the discovery that there are certain future outcomes which are more or less independent of the 'shape of the future' where other outcomes are highly tied to particular sets of assumptions or other outcomes. If we accept that the future is not predetermined, then I argue that a core value of education can be found in the famous prayer

> God grant me the serenity
> To accept the things I cannot change;
> Courage to change the things I can;
> And wisdom to know the difference.

If a child leaving school had the ability to understand and live the above sentiment that would be more powerful in my estimation than any specific qualification.

My experience is that sometimes people try to create the ideal scenario and a bad scenario. This is in my opinion a mistake. Similarly in technological futures, I often find a desire to 'change everything' in contradiction to my first observation. The value of scenarios in my experience lies in them being plausible rather than utopian or dystopian. Of course my utopia might well be your dystopia.

What I still find amusing after many years about the works of Douglas Adams is that he combines the advances of technology with bumbling humans. This feels more real than those stories where we see humans whose lives and emotions have little link to us. For those stories to be true, my second observation would be wrong.

4 The future never evolves the way we think, or at the pace we think

When I was 10, the promise of controlled fission, of limitless cheap electricity, was thought to be ten years away. At the time of writing I am 56. I am not holding my breath! Another conceit is the 'no one could have foreseen that' argument. At the time of writing, this argument is frequently made about the credit crunch. My own experience is that when you look back there are individuals who did get it right. Often they were ignored or dismissed as peripheral. Those who spotted the looming credit crunch were dismissed because they could not create quantitative models which proved their point. What has unfurled is that their criticisms were of the slavish belief in quantitative models.

Another important element is to realize that a 'trend is a trend until it bends'. Often trends in particular areas may contradict others. This interaction of different trends may produce uncertainty or counter-intuitive results.

For instance, the life expectancy in the Western world has been growing steadily decade by decade. It is forecast to do so going forward. At the same time there is concern of a growing 'obesity epidemic' which will potentially take years off people's lives. This is expected to become more serious over the next few decades. Now put those together –will we live longer or not? If we tackle the obesity issue will life expectancy grow faster? If we fail to tackle obesity will increasing longevity slow or reverse? The next issue, then, is to look at health inequalities in this context. There is clear evidence to show that there is a large gap in life expectancy associated with poverty. The scale of the obesity challenge is also interrelated with inequality. If we reduce income inequalities that may well feed through into changes to the obesity challenge, life expectancy and, in turn, to a challenge for pension funding. I hope that this illustrates the complexity of forecasting virtually anything.

All I can advise is that when you hear an argument that dogmatically claims that we will see a life expectancy for men of 93 years by 2050, there are an awful lot of assumptions behind that. I would observe that often these claims do not make those assumptions explicit and can be taken with a good dose of salt.

5 Framing the question and who you ask is harder than you think

I would like to illustrate this with an example in education. If we look at the number of jobs in the economy that require confidence and skills in IT then it is quite clear that 'IT literacy' is fast becoming an essential part of work and society.

So, what do you need to teach a 5 year old so that he or she will be IT literate when they reach 20?

In the last 20 years a typical computer has become 1,000 times faster, has 200 times the storage capacity and 500 times the communications capabilities for the same price. There is still an expectation that the same level of change can occur in the next 20 years. Remember my point 4 above. Your judgement is likely to be no better or worse than the experts if this will be turn out to be true. More of that later.

In 1980 you wouldn't have asked Oracle or Microsoft, now the two largest software companies in the world, as they were small players at the time. The IBM PC was 1981, so you would have missed that too. In 1990 you wouldn't have asked CISCO, a giant of the networking world, and you would have missed the World Wide Web which was still sitting at CERN in Geneva. So, to answer that from an IT perspective is tricky enough. Who might know from an education and skills perspective? If you asked a primary teacher or an employer how would you know how to judge their suggestions?

I know plenty of people who have a variety of opinions. One of them will probably turn out to be right, but I'm not sure I could successfully bet on which one. Remember that I argued that the 'couldn't have been foreseen' argument is frequently flawed. What is undoubtedly hard is to work out who has insight and who is barking mad.

So, armed with my five principles above, how might we construct a view of the shape of the future to inform our thinking?

My experience is that, when you largely don't know where you are and where you are going, what is needed is resilience. In these circumstances, what tends to guide our decisions are our values and beliefs, individually and collectively. So, my hypothesis for the shaping the future is that the starting point is to create a sufficiently rich framework of values and beliefs within which the actions of individuals, communities, companies and governments are likely to be worked out. In turn this framework should be developed, supported by what evidence can be found, mindful of the five principles outlined earlier. We can then look at the constraints and drivers we believe may impact the possible futures we can consider.

I make no special claim for my personal framework, but offer it based on my own experience. Please feel free to build your own or to modify mine for your own purposes. I have tested these ideas over a decade in a number of countries in public and private sectors with differing political environments.

The set of values and beliefs I propose is as follows:

a   Economic competitiveness with social inclusion
b   Risk: Management vs minimization
c   Life-long learning for all
d   Social innovation over technological invention
e   'Smallish' is beautiful
f   Interdependence over independence
g   Value added with values

It is important to accept that values espoused and values acted on may be different. Understanding these gaps and tensions may help us understand what we might aspire to but also the resource constraints, which limit our ability to fully accomplish those goals. Let me briefly explain this set.

a   Different countries have different approaches and different dynamics when it comes to economic performance. If we observe the ratio of incomes from the top and bottom decile then we can see great variations between, say, Scandinavia and the USA. Some will argue that inequality drives innovation and economic performance and creates the resources that, in turn, fund social progress. Others will point out that the more unequal a society the greater the costs that society bears in terms of poor health and education, crime and social cohesion. There is a growing body of evidence that as income per capita rises then the overall benefit to a society in terms of increased happiness, for instance, diminishes and is badly impacted by inequality. Societies with high prison populations are often associated with poor educational standards in the lower deciles.

b   I argue that good entrepreneurs manage risk, poor entrepreneurs take risks and bureaucrats tend to minimize or eliminate risk. Life is full of risks. They cannot be eliminated. Yet we find governments increasingly expected to guarantee that societies do not face risks. Climate change, for instance, contains many serious risks for our whole planet and our species. While there is an impressive scientific consensus on the evidence for global warming, the collective ability to manage risks is lacking.

c   One of the key changes in the latter half of the last century has been a rate of economic change that has largely eliminated jobs for life and impacted many careers and professions. We can no longer expect a population to have the skills and competencies when they leave school, college or university to guarantee a full adult life of work. The extent to which we, as individuals, or our society embrace notions of lifelong learning will impact on economic performance, quality of life and social cohesion.

d   Science and technology developments will continue to provide a basis for economic and social progress. However, it is not just about inventing new drugs in medicine, low-carbon technologies or new IT capabilities, but the organizational and cultural arrangements we make to exploit these new potentials. An historical example is the creation of the BBC in the UK; a new institutional form needed to 'democratize' access to radio and TV. Scientists in stem cell research talk about the future potential of personalized medicines, offering greater efficacy and reduced side effects. If, and when, this happens, will this be available to the rich or to all?

e   The industrial society saw economies of scale as key to efficiency. Our awareness of the resource constraints of our planet and new knowledge working models has made us more aware of some diseconomies of scale. The insolvency of General Motors illustrates how hard it is for large organizations to adapt to changing technologies and markets. When we look at countries similar effects can be seen. Singapore, Finland and other Scandinavian economies, for instance, have shown a greater facility for absorbing technology progress.

At the same time, not everything can be done bottom up or on small scale. To give everyone access to broadband networks, electricity, telephone networks or roads requires top level co-ordination or policy. It is less a question of centralization vs decentralization as doing top down what needs to be done top down and doing bottom up what is most effective.

f   As we grow up, we move from being dependent on our parents and other adults, to become (hopefully) independent adults. However, that is not the end of the journey. Marriage, children and families create the challenge, in turn, of mutual dependence and interdependence. Similarly, the changing economies require companies to work collaboratively with others. In some industries this includes cooperation with competitors. I can argue that English schools and FE colleges moved from a position of being dependent on their local authorities to becoming independent bodies. I do not think we have yet fully explored educational interdependence. Our ability to mitigate and handle the consequences of environmental change and resource constraints will, I am sure, be dependent on our ability to move from being independent players to recognizing and managing our interdependence at many levels.

g   Many in business used to argue that the sole reason for businesses was to make money. The growth of corporate social responsibility and environmental awareness have increased the pressure from stakeholders on business. I recognize that many organizations have not moved beyond lip service, but the power of NGOs, media and the new social media to campaign against 'gloss without substance' has been growing for years. I think the trend will last for many years, but how far organizations can be brought to heel is difficult to generalize from high-profile cases.

Now let us turn to the drivers of change. One of the commonly used frameworks is PESTEL (Political, Economic, Social, Environmental and Legislative). In this framework, the drivers of change are organized against these six dimensions of change.

In most models, factors such as globalization of the economy, the ageing population in the developed world, consumerism, urbanization and scientific advances are considered. One model that I have found useful is the 21 drivers of change for the twenty-first century from a specialist consultancy Outsights. Their comprehensive model can be found at www.outsights.co.uk.

Whichever model you choose or whichever drivers you consider, I have found it useful to use the framework of values and beliefs as a lens to test assumptions and to enrich the scenario development.

To round this chapter off let me illustrate my approach by looking at a specific futures question: which languages will it be important for children to learn if Britain is to be successful in the twenty-first century?

We can use the value framework to define the components of success, be they political, economic, social or environmental, for instance. The increasing global integration of the world economy, on the one hand, looks good for English-speaking countries. However, looking at the likely key languages, I would argue that Chinese, the major Asian languages, notably of India, would figure highly. The growth of Brazil and other Latin and South American countries puts a premium on Spanish and Portuguese. Also, if we think through the value framework, we can rethink some of our contemporary challenges.

Is it a problem to have 80-plus languages spoken in a London school or is it a huge opportunity? My analysis is that if we see and manage each school as an independent entity, resources constraints will emphasize the problem. However, if we see schools as interdependent entities in a system of learning then they can exploit each other's wealth of resources to create opportunities not yet realized. The use of networking technologies enables that sharing and interdependence in ways which a generation ago would have sounded like science fiction.

It is easy to build exciting visions of a future based on new possibilities. What I have argued here is that it is engagement with those futures that is the challenge. Alan Kay, a leading light of the IT industry, once said 'the best way to predict the future is to invent it'. I think he's right and we can go further.

Don't ask where technological and economic change will take us. That treats the future in a deterministic way. Start with the following: 'If we could build the future we want, what would it look like?' Look at the future through the lens of values and beliefs. It doesn't guarantee success, nothing does. For me, it makes the journey more interesting and purposeful. We can help to shape the future. A hard road maybe, but in words made famous last year, 'Can we fix it? Yes we can'.

3 Global economics and the nature of work

Richard Crabtree

What we do for a living is affected by our education

What most people do for a living, certainly in the twentieth and early twenty-first centuries, seems to follow on from educational choices made in their teens or early 20s. As the challenges of an increasingly fast-changing economy demand increasing flexibility in terms of skills, knowledge and capability, there will be an ever increasing focus on life-long learning to facilitate that flexibility. Thus, a successful education system must not just produce qualified 'end products', but must provide its students with the life skills to be able to ensure they do not become obsolete.

For many people, when they were young children their perception of what people did all day long seemed very simple. Being a carpenter, a nurse, a teacher or a train-driver seemed easy to understand and many children aspired to be those things. The education system gave them the necessary skills to set out on a path to fulfil one of those roles. They hoped that the education and vocational training they undertook would provide them with certainty and a regular income that would supply their needs. It would also fund their social life and provide them with meaning and significance.

What we do for a living is key to our identity. It's one of the first things we find out about each other, but most jobs are now so specialized that we need to ask about five questions before we know what somebody actually does. Not many children aspired to be a project manager, business systems analyst or a fleet and facilities manager. However, many of them will fulfil such a role at some point in their career. They made choices in terms of subjects and specialization in their education with a very simplistic view of the roles that they could perform.

Most people's jobs became specialized because it was the easiest way of becoming more efficient, which in turn facilitated the growth necessary to keep economies moving forward in the traditional sense. It is also a widely held belief that as jobs became more specialized they became less satisfying to do.

What we do fits within a wider economy

Given that the world of work involves some form of engagement with the economy and one of the key roles of education is to prepare people for that world, it is worth considering whether the education system is fit for purpose or whether it churns out a random proportion of engineers, factory workers, doctors, accountants and systems analysts into an economy that may not require their services 20 years down the line.

What is the nature of work in a post-industrial society?

If society becomes largely knowledge-based what becomes of artisans and unskilled manual labour? Can life-long learning be sustained? If the nature of work changes radically can education be divorced from the demand to generate skills for employment?

Anyone glancing through the first few pages of any business-focused book written in the last 25 years will almost certainly come across the expression: 'the world of business is in turmoil as never before', followed by a description of how we got into that situation and how to deal with it. The macroeconomic world has lurched between *laissez faire* policies, which allowed the market to make the crucial decisions regarding the allocation of resources and various flavours of interventionist policies. We are in a world of discontinuous change. This is a key feature of a post-modern world.

It is worth looking at the economic and business environment and how we got to where we are. According to Alain de Botton, in *The Pleasures and Sorrows of Work* (2009), the world of work in the UK changed sometime around the mid eighteenth century. Incidentally, he also points out that attitudes in the sphere of romance also changed around that time too. Essentially, he explains that two of the most important life decisions used to be simple. To paraphrase, if your father was a baker you became a baker. Whom you married was decided upon by convenience and expedience. Until then the son of a carpenter didn't become a world leader, because the opportunity wasn't available and it wasn't deemed to be his station in life You didn't marry for love; you married so the family land or cooking pot would be handed down to your descendents in the proper way. From the mid 1700s onwards the idea arose that you could do something that you were good at and that fulfilled you and that your spouse could be someone you loved.

He also goes on to say that these two changes have helped make everybody miserable, by raising their expectations unreasonably high. It led to the twin thoughts that you could enjoy your job and you could live happily ever after with your spouse. The environment in which we all try to make a living has certainly changed from the days when you know who had baked your bread; who made and sold you the candles with which you lit your house. Everybody knew that you did what you did for a living. All those jobs either relieved someone's suffering or improved their life in some other way. We gained satisfaction from that. A systems analyst analyzes systems and probably has no idea if their work is even taken into any consideration at all. Which it probably is not!

Essentially, the world of business is the micro-environment which functions within the macro environment. For those of us in the UK, that currently means some form of capitalism.

Economies bring uncertainty – models have been tried to bring stability, but they do not succeed

When Francis Fukuyama declared the 'end of history' in *The End of History and the Last Man* in 1989 after the demise of the Berlin Wall and all it stood for, he was claiming the success of capitalism as an ideology over communism. It was envisaged that a capitalist future would lead us to sustained growth and stability, some form of certainty. It seemed that there was no argument any more between the planned economies and those that were market led. Adam Smith had been proved right after all; individuals act in everyone's interest when they put their own interests first and this theory had won out. What followed was a continuation of an economic theme that had grown more influential in the West since the mid 1970s.

Only time will tell whether the economic downturn in the late Noughties will compare with the Great Depression of the 1930s, though the causes are depressingly similar. The outcomes may differ because the world's leaders may have actually learnt how to resolve the problem from mistakes made by previous administrations (though they certainly hadn't learnt how to avoid the situation in the first place). Essentially, the history of economics tells us that the market had held sway. Libertarians would argue the market wasn't free enough and economists from the left would say it was too uncontrolled.

From the late eighteenth century, the Industrial Revolution in the UK and North-western Europe launched the world into unprecedented economic change and growth. This was facilitated by the philosophical change in people's perception of work and the increasing specialization of jobs.

This economic growth and the nature of how people worked within the economy was studied by a growing group of intellectuals including Adam Smith, David Ricardo and Karl Marx. They looked at how this growth might best be continued. Thomas Malthus was one economist who concluded that this could not be successfully achieved. He argued that as wages increase within an economy, effectively increasing the average wealth of a population, the death rate will tend to decrease (due to better diet and general health care) and the surviving birth rate will tend to increase (as children are an economic good and wealth leads to more children). This would in turn, therefore, increase the supply of labour, which would drive the wages down again, with the resultant increase in death rates and fall in birth rates, resulting in no growth in the population and, ultimately, the elimination of growth in the economy.

Adam Smith wrote in *The Wealth of Nations* that the pursuit of enlightened self-interest by individuals and companies benefits society as a whole. Perhaps his most widely known quote is:

> It is not from the benevolence of the butcher, the brewer, or the baker that we expect our dinner, but from their regard to their own self-interest. We address ourselves, not to their humanity but to their self-love, and never talk to them of our own necessities but of their advantages.(Smith, 1776: page 18)

Although this does seem to speak of the individual having a rather 'me first' attitude, he actually considered society as something which should benefit and be central to an individual's decisions.

Ricardo introduced the concept of comparative advantage, still a fundamental concept in trade theory. It is one of the essential elements of free trade between economies and, importantly for this discussion, for specialization among individuals. His case is that there is benefit to both parties from an exchange or trade as long as each one delivers something where they have relative productivity advantage.

So an individual with a surplus of cash and a blocked drain, but little appetite for getting his hands dirty unblocking the drain is happy to trade some cash in return for another person who has need of cash and the willingness to get his hands dirty.

These thinkers led to an understanding of economics that went largely unchallenged for some time, partly because it was a new study and partly because the theories supporting this free trade did seem to explain what was observed. They also did seem to work, but to whose benefit?

The huge growth in the UK economy during the Industrial Revolution, in particular, brought huge wealth to some. Others began to question the use of the profits being made. Karl Marx was one of the first to fully appreciate that investment of profit into new factories and new technologies would support continued growth. Until then, this economic development was considered to be a phenomenon that might disappear as quickly as it appeared. If the link between those two elements broke down, growth would falter. Marx also first identified the business cycle, and the boom and bust which we are all now so familiar with.

The situation in the first decades of the twentieth century was ever changing. New economies were emerging and the political landscape was restless. The UK was overtaken by Germany and the US in terms of economic power. There was an economic boom that both these export-led manufacturing economies benefited from. The result of this rapid growth was that by the late 1920s massive over-borrowing on the latest technologies, steam ships and railways had taken place. A post-war Europe looked potentially set to default on its payments, confidence crashed and numerous banks, the mainstay of the economic system, collapsed.

Marx had laid the foundations for a different way of managing an economy and Russia was the first to try it. These planned economies, notably the USSR, were actually coping rather better with the economic downturn in the 1930s. Perhaps the free market needed some of its freedom curtailed. Most agreed that something different was needed. The first time a wide range of independent nations agreed to maintain an agreed economic arrangement, ostensibly aimed at solving the problems of the 1930s depression and the world war that followed, was agreed at Bretton Woods in 1944.

This agreement committed the developed economies involved to a fixed exchange rate between their currencies and effectively to try to contain the wildest excesses of the market.

In a global economy with individual national currencies, trade relies on the fact that those currencies are freely convertible. One of the key themes of the Bretton Woods conference was that the freely floating rates in the 1930s had been too unstable and that these monetary fluctuations caused the stalling of free trade.

In the absence of a central government or single currency, a structure was set up whereby the World Bank and the International Monetary Fund managed a system of fixed exchange rates using the US as a reserve currency.

The Bretton Woods agreement led to what became known as Keynesian economics and introduced a structure which some believed would provide the answers while others believed it would produce more problems.

Out of this situation, a new economic paradigm emerged where intervention from the state during the downturn in the economic cycle was an acceptable solution. Employment was seen as a right and structures were put in place to ensure that there was full employment. Set numbers of engineers, doctors and factory workers were produced by the education system.

The free market, or classical economics, had been judged to have failed, so some form of structure was applied to the running of all economies for a large part of the twentieth century. Most of the West adhered to some form of Keynesian economic thought. A planned economy or a group of economies tied into a formal structure as set up by Bretton Woods or as the European Union was instituted after the Second World War, inevitably interfered with one of the most fundamental relationships in economics; demand and supply.

Two things happened in the 1970s. In 1971 the US decided they would not allow the dollar to be the 'gold standard' currency and a trebling of the price of oil just three years later caused a massive disruption. The market was having its say again. At a microeconomic level, there was a surge in unemployment following the oil shocks and the effective collapse of Keynesian principles. Was this caused by the prevailing economic thought, or because education hadn't changed and was still producing the same people with the same skills in the same proportion? Put more simply, did the workforce have anything that those with money wanted to buy?

So, the mid 1970s brought economic shocks in the form of a trebling of oil prices, coupled with the end of a technological era based on oil-burning vehicles, from trains and planes to automobiles. That technology had facilitated relatively rapid global communication which had begun the globalization of business and led to the growth in the multi-national corporation.

It's noticeable that since the mid 1970s the nature of earnings, always unequal but at least with both top and bottom of the ladder increasing at the same percentage rate year on year, began to change.

Globalization has brought a new challenge to everyone trying to earn a living in the twenty-first century. The people who dealt with our airline ticket and banking enquiries used to be on the high street. Then they were on the end of the phone in a central office in every town. In a global economy they were now likely to be in a call centre in development areas in the UK and subsequently in India and the Far East. Essentially, because the nature of what someone did for you became more specialized and the physical location of the person carrying that task out became physically irrelevant, someone who would work for less took the job from the person in the local high street.

If one assumes a hierarchy of jobs, for instance in a bank, from contact centre agent, through cashier in a branch, right up to the chief executive in head office, there has been an increasing drive to reduce the costs at the bottom of the ladder, while those on the higher rungs have earned increasingly more. Those at the top of the ladder began to climb higher and faster, while those at the bottom were kept there by others joining the bottom rungs.

Moving up and down that ladder may be termed a measure of social mobility. Many commentators have previously thought social mobility was purely due to education. It seemed self-evident that someone with a good education would be likely to gain entry to a more highly paid job. Someone with a degree in accountancy would be more likely to be a leader in a company than someone with an A level in accountancy. However, the increasing gap in earnings from top to bottom has been facilitated by the increase in leverage those leaders had over their predecessors. The boss may have been called MD in the 1970s; today they may call themselves Global CEO. Essentially the same job in the UK, but multiplied perhaps 100 times if the company operates in 100 countries. This has been facilitated by the developments in communications, effectively increasing the influence one individual can have, and therefore increasing their rewards.

The MD of a company in one country may have been very successful in the national market, but as economic barriers were lowered by free trade agreements and economic zones, that company had a choice: stay national or look to increase business internationally. Those who succeeded in this defeated or swallowed up the losers and that MD became global president of a global company, with far more power, influence and reward than previously. The prize became bigger, for both the company and the leader of the company. So, also, the nature of work changed for those lower down the ladder.

Education and career opportunities

It seems reasonable to expect that, with the increases in expenditure on state education in the UK since the 1970s, access to the top universities, very often the door that facilitates entry to the 'top jobs' in organizations, would become increasingly open to those from comprehensives rather than public schools. What has happened, according to Paul Ormerod in *Why Most Things Fail* (2005), is the opposite. Admissions from the state sector increased after the Second World War up until the late 1970s. At this point state system pupils made up two-thirds of admissions to Oxford and Cambridge.

Since then, the trend has changed sharply and there have been markedly fewer admissions from the state sector, despite positive admission policies from the universities themselves. Ormerod states that fewer and fewer appear able to compete at the highest level and so advance themselves economically and socially.

Some would argue that this trend is simply a function of Western society. The evidence, however, is that the inequality gap is widest in Brazil, followed by the US, then China, then France and the UK. Germany and Sweden were the most evenly distributed, along with South Korea and India (Deninger and Squire World Bank Inequality Database; Ormerod: page 43).

John Harvey-Jones in *All Together Now* (1994) stated that something in the psychology of the British blocked them from the view held by those from the US and Germany, that they are capable of doing any job in an organization, including that of leader of the organization. Education would seem the best way to counter this view by raising aspirations and potential together with a preparation for the job, should the opportunity arise.

Considering education purely in the sense of how it can benefit an economy, that is, by creating suitable producer-consumers, what end goal needs to be reached by an individual in an educational sense?

Would this be facilitated by an increase in spending in education? The Chinese economy has been one of the world's economic success stories since the late 1970s. It's interesting to note that all vocational training in China was stopped during the Cultural Revolution (it was believed to encourage bourgeois skills) and was only re-established in the late 1970s. No teachers were trained until 1971, universities had to wait for new admissions until 1972 and there were no post-graduates until 1978. The rapid economic growth of China has coincided with the opening up of the doors to education. There were many other social and political factors. On the face of it growth and education seem inexorably linked. Countries with similar incomes spend an average of 3.4 per cent of GDP (Hutton 2007: page 168), whereas China spends only 2 per cent. Hutton goes on to state, however, that literacy and numeracy in China have slipped back since Mao. Great progress was made in these areas between 1949 and 1976 but are now due to fail to meet expected targets by 2015.

Increasingly, the employee has taken the risk of employment. The benefits offered to workers in the UK are ever more focused on those that do not commit the company long term. We see pensions moving from being a defined benefit to becoming a defined contribution and there is an increase in the volume of contractor-type jobs. Charles Handy identified this as a trend in the 1980s and it is becoming still more apparent. Thus it becomes more incumbent on the workers to ensure they are trained, rather than on the company, which previously may have offered a job for life, with retraining as appropriate.

Who should pay for life-long learning?

The direct beneficiaries, the individual undertaking the learning? Or the indirect beneficiaries, the employer, the government or society?

Can you add value by your physical labour anymore or is it what you know, how you know it, how you do it, and less what you do now? If a role cannot be outsourced to another country, you could be safe, but migrant workers have always posed a threat, especially to the unskilled. Even highly skilled workers have always been under threat from being undercut by hardworking, flexible, mobile workers.

The successful have always had a head start – education is key to this. How does it need to change to ensure we are not a nation of labourers that have to match Chinese labour rates (but actually cannot)? What are the future industries? Is a software programme more valuable than a pop single or a film or TV programme? Surely it's all content and people will pay for its benefits?

During a period of history in which world political leaders have dallied with the free market as well as a variety of forms of planned economy and found each method and ideology wanting, has the education system changed, or is it still effectively recycling traditional formats of provision?

Paul Ormerod in a speech in May 2005 at the Bristol Festival of Ideas commented on the challenge posed where anyone who could beat a chicken pecking 'randomly' at noughts and crosses would win $5,000. Apparently they paid out only once. He suggests that noughts and crosses is a simple game. Chess is a complicated game with far more variations which are harder to understand and this control and that business are far more complicated still, with all the myriad variations causing success and failure, so can anyone plan for a business or an economy?

He went on to say that planning cannot work, but that innovation and flexibility should be encouraged.

If that is true, which method of education has proved most successful may be a better philosophy to pursue than economic ideology. It would appear to be the ones that have provided innovators, entrepreneurs and skilled workers and in these in right proportion. Education and up-skilling of individuals within an economy, by that economy.

Given that the answer to that question varies depending on which part of history one considers, perhaps there is no one answer. Or perhaps it is the case that all systems may have their time, and the trick is to eliminate or improve upon the systems which fail. Economically, maintaining a system that was initiated for factory-based production or seasonal working makes little if any sense in a global economy being driven by new technologies and business paradigms.

An advert in the *Guardian* newspaper (27 May 2009) put this succinctly: 'I want to be in new media. So you just can't teach in the same old way'.

4 Value added: learning to make people thicker

Russell Rook

Introduction

Why me? This was my first thought when invited to contribute a chapter to this book. While obviously honoured by the invite, this is the first time that I've been asked to contribute to a volume on education. Upon reflection there are two, possibly mutually inclusive, answers to my initial question. First, while never having trained as a teacher, a good deal of my professional life has been spent working with young people, schools, educationalists and policy-makers. Secondly, my academic work deals with many of the issues that this chapter is seeking to address. And so now for a more formal introduction, my name is Russell Rook and I am a theologian.

My task here is to consider the subject of values, an area of endless fascination and significant common ground between educators and theologians. Religious congregations and educational institutions are among the organizations most likely to ascribe to formal set of values. As with any ethos-driven community, these values statements provide both the common denominator and the supreme goal of the community's life. In *Values in Education and Education in Values,* Mark Halstead (1995) defines values schemes as

> principles, fundamental convictions, ideals, standards or life stances which act as general guides to behaviour or as reference points in decision-making or the evaluation of beliefs or action. (page 5)

Upon close examination a values scheme demonstrates how an individual or organization views the world. They represent both the things that they hold dear and the things that they hope for. It is surely not too much to say that, in outlining a set of values, organizations, whether religious or secular, mark out some form of sacred space. In this space, through important patterns of behaviour, shared beliefs and communal aspirations, we discover what makes an organization or community identifiable and distinct.

While surveying the common ground, this chapter will also identify some of the differences between educationalists and theologians when it comes to the subject of values. Theologians far more eminent than I have been heard to rail against the values machine. Whether philosophically or practically, theoretically or theologically, values schemes can be rendered problematic. Below we will outline three particular challenges. First, the question of origination, or where values schemes come from. Secondly, the challenge of pragmatism. Here we will address the limitations of a purely pragmatic approach to values schemes. Thirdly, we will highlight the role that personal choice plays in the failure or success of different values scheme. Not resting content with the questions and challenges, in each case we will press on and address the real opportunities that values schemes provide to enhance and transform educational communities.

Keep taking the tablets: the challenge of origination

Having pictured Zarathustra breaking the sacred tablets, the Judaeo/Christian symbols of divine revelation, Nietzche famously announced that 'God had died!' From here on it would fall to mankind to decide what was 'valuable' and subsequently live in accordance with those decisions. It is not hard to see why the origins of values-speak cause some theologians to twitch. That said, it is not the nihilistic source of the scheme that is most troubling. There are more pressing problems to address.

Following Nietzche's lead, the first challenge concerns how we calculate what is valuable in the first place. Given the sometimes oppressive track records of certain religious communities, who justify the unjustifiable with a nod in the direction of a supposedly 'divine' revelation, one can sympathize with Zarathustra. And yet the aftermath leaves us with a dilemma. If our values rest only upon what we determine as valuable as a community, then a community's beliefs and aspirations may at best be the result of an election and, at worst, the personal preference of a charismatic leader. The influence of Nietzche upon Hitler has been remarked upon often and hardly needs restating here. That said, having yet to come across an educational institution suppressing the masses through its values scheme, I wish to raise a more general and persistent problem. In a society which no longer holds one single divine revelation in common, where should our values originate from?

As is often the case, finding an answer to this question requires us to ask a set of subsequent questions. To this end, when faced with a values-driven organization, I make the following enquiries: Whose values are they anyway? What authority did the decision-makers have or exercise in making these values? What processes determined the values in the first place and what were the major philosophical inputs? By asking these questions it should become possible to identify origins of the scheme. That said, I can remember only a few occasions when answers have been readily available, let alone intellectually satisfying. Here we arrive at the one of this single greatest challenges facing values-driven organizations. In truth, these organizations often do not think deeply, either proactively or reactively, about the origins of their own values, despite the fact that the failure to do so jeopardizes the values scheme altogether.

The occasions when I have received satisfactory answer to these question have usually coincided with a visit to an exemplary educational establishment. Asking these same questions here, one soon discovers that both staff and students are clearly aware of the reasons, stories, traditions and origins of their particular set of values. While not necessarily on the original committee, the whole community knows that certain virtues and behaviours are essential aspects of the school's history, life together and future direction. In short, the community know where their values come from and choose to appropriate them for themselves, making the community's history into their story. On occasion this may result from a school's connection to a faith tradition, distinctive founding stories, the particular history of the local community and/or a particular strategic focus of school life. Either way, the fact that the community understands where these values come from enables them to realize them in the present and persist with them into the future. In short, the school's values hold the key to both the belonging and becoming of the community as a whole.

In one London school I came across the headteacher commissioned a team of senior students to create a set of values for the whole school. Having researched the history of the institution, the students interviewed fellow students, staff, parents and community members. Following this consultation period the students were invited to present their findings and recommendations to the student body, staff and governors. From here they were commissioned to work on an implementation plan and the chair of the group was appointed and paid to oversee this process during her gap year. A full-time ambassador of the school's values programme, she was responsible for making sure that the school's values became the driving force in every aspect of school life. In this capacity she had the authority to challenge any area of policy or procedure that she believed contradicted the beliefs and aspirations that unified the school. Given this example, it is easy to see how a careful process of values origination and subsequent implementation can radically increase the impact of the overall scheme.

While many organizations have values, few, in my experience, are driven by them in the same way as above. Part of the reason for this is that leaders find it too easy to circumvent the process by which an authentic and meaningful set of values are originated. Following Nietzche, it takes a good degree of work for men and women to work out what a community finds truly valuable and why. If this work remains undone our values schemes are likely only to remain as print on a poster or copy in a prospectus. However, if we are prepared to press on the most remarkable transformations may become possible. And so now, we press on.

Not so stoic: The challenge of the pragmatic

When asking about the process of origination, one cannot help but conclude that many leaders are fiercely pragmatic when it comes to the creation of values schemes. For most of us who struggle under the burden of a heavy work load pragmatism is an all together attractive doctrine. After all, 'getting the job done' is no mean feat. However, while practical in the short term, pragmatism can be hugely dispiriting in the long run. Put simply, pragmatism doesn't offer us much to live for aside from getting out of bed in the morning. I recently sat with a community leader and public service provider who, through tired and frustrated eyes, outlined the vision he had cast at the outset of his career only to confess that 25 years on he had achieved very little. Why had this not been possible? Because it took everything he had to get the basic job done. In short, he started out as an excited visionary and ended up as a disillusioned pragmatist.

One of the single greatest problems of value schemes in education is their failure to raise the levels of human aspiration and achievement. An overly pragmatic approach to values is in part to blame. Overly pragmatic values schemes tend towards a contractual approach. The reason we need values, they seem to suggest, is simply to provide frameworks for human behaviours and interactions. These schemes present both what is acceptable – if you want to be part of our gang you can't do that – and ideological – if you want to be an authentic part of this community you should try this. Here we list the essential procedures and protocols for those wishing to be part of the community.

A long time ago I was a youth worker. Back in the day we regularly used one particular values exercise with our young people. As another unruly bunch turned up for youth club at the start of a new term, one of us would grab a flip-chart and ask them to list the values that they wished to live by in sessions to come. Upon reflection, this exercise had real potential to transform young people's lives. However back then, it was a purely a pragmatic tool to insight appropriate behaviour. The reason we facilitated the exercise was to create a process whereby the young people themselves could outline and enforce the rules of the club and as a result make our work more manageable.

Overly pragmatic values schemes often default to the procedural. Put simply they declare 'this is how we do it round here!' As a result they may help us keep the peace but often fail to achieve long-term change in terms of a student's character. Along these lines, the American ethicist, Stanley Hauerwas (2001) draws an interesting distinction between the disciples of Aristotle and their contemporaries, the Stoics. Both groups, by and large, believed in the classical virtues of the ancient world: temperance, prudence, fortitude and justice. However, Hauerwas suggests, for the Stoics these virtues, while important, were largely about presentation. To this end, a Stoic would declare that they adhered to a certain principle or made certain choices because that was what was expected in their community and culture. For the Stoics virtues were contractual and procedural. The Aristotelians on the other hand, did not see their virtues as mere procedure or presentation but rather as a character trait to be learned and acquired over many years. For an Aristotelian, a virtuous character was not simply someone who acknowledged what was just and made personal choices in line with this. A virtuous man was someone who had become utterly and habitually just having spent years in training and learning.

Hauerwas' parable intersects well with our current conversation. An educator's vision for learning surely stretches beyond teaching students to simply obey the laws or even the making of good choices. The educators that impact the most are the ones whose work have transformative impact on a student's life. While they certainly facilitate the acquisition of knowledge, more importantly they inform and influence the growth and development of personal identity. As human identity is far from static, particularly in the formative years, educators fulfil this essential role in the lives of human beings, or should we say human becomings. Where values are concerned, the role of educators is not simply to teach desired procedures or contractual obligations but rather to help students develop real character and virtue.

A pupil referral unit I once worked with received a substantial amount of money with which to run a bicycle design and maintenance project. Having found a friendly volunteer to run the programme, a handful of teenage boys was referred to attend ten sessions. On day one they were introduced to the equipment and told that over the next ten weeks they would design their own mountain bike worth over £100. As they darted out of the centre that night the only discussion was as to how fast they could sell the finished bikes and for what price. Following the final session, as the boys wheeled their new bikes out of the building, not one mention was made about the prospect of profiteering from their labour. Where the boys were concerned, the real value of their bikes had increased exponentially, to the point where they simply could not be monetized. Upon completion the bikes became crowning symbols of all they had been through together. They were now almost priceless and in this afforded the boys a new opportunity to learn and grow; for some time after, the group regularly went mountain biking with the volunteer.

While the group never agreed a set of values at the commencement of the course, the process resulted in the young people radically re-evaluating their notions of what was valuable. At the start they valued a possible income stream. At the end they valued the experience of learning together and developing skills in an inclusive community. Their decisions changed radically and naturally. Hence the programme not only provided the boys with a new sense of value but helped them to build character and discover virtue. In this they achieved something I never achieved through those flip-chart sessions at the youth club. Twenty-first century education requires values systems that stretch beyond the bounds of pragmatism and enable young people to build character and virtue. Understood and implemented well, such a values scheme has the power to transform both the choices students make and, more importantly, the students who make the choices.

Making schools thicker: The challenge of choice

Having addressed the importance of origins and pushed beyond the bounds of pragmatism, we come to the third challenge facing values schemes. Here we come up against the potentially problematic role of choice. Regardless of how well a community devises and implements a set of values, the simple fact remains that unless individuals choose to personally appropriate the scheme, the project is in vain. To this end, the success of a values scheme lie as much in the act of another's interpretation as it does in the community's origination or communication. Try as we might there is simply no way around this.

I once belonged to a church congregation that valued transformation, celebration and simplicity. Being a rabid activist I was happy to sign up to the first. Enjoying the occasional party, especially as a celebration of some activity or achievement, I proved pretty good at the second. However, having grown accustomed to creature comforts and, as with many an academic, being wedded to complexity, I found the final simplicity very hard. Hence, I engaged at best tokenistically and occasionally used intellectual devices to feign alignment. The point being that as a member of the community my personal choices had the potential to confirm, ignore or deny the congregation's values.

Presuming that none of us wish to mitigate against the rights of an individual to choose a set of values, the question arises as to how we make it easier for people to understand and/or buy into a values scheme. In my experience, the main reason that an individual chooses to ignore or reject a value is not because they are opposed to the concept. I know of few people who do not value inclusion, respect, kindness, generosity, freedom, transformation, etc. The real reason why individuals struggle to appropriate certain values is because, by their nature, values are often hard to understand and apply.

The challenge of values reception is heightened in a school setting. Here, a values scheme often involves a list of what, upon reflection, are highly abstract and esoteric terms. Terms such as respect, inclusion, freedom, etc. are not easy concepts to define, let alone apply. These terms are categorical terms, used to summarize a range of virtues, beliefs, behaviours and actions under one concept. If we were to ask ten adults to define 'inclusion' we would be sure to receive ten different definitions, some of which may contradict. Likewise a group of philosophers or theologians could, and do, spend hours contesting each other's use of the terms. Given this challenge, how are educators to help students understand and embody certain values?

Stanley Hauerwas comes to our aid again. Faced with this challenge, Hauerwas (2001) talks about the need to 'thicken' a word or a concept. Let's return to the word 'inclusion'. Using Hauerwas' model, rather than narrowing a term to a final definition or conceptual common denominator, we seek to 'thicken' it by adding layers of meaning and interpretation. We can achieve this in a number of ways. We can tell stories that illustrate inclusion in action, develop habits and rituals which enforce regular acts of inclusion, express inclusion through art and creativity, conduct reading, research and conversation around the theme and look to the distinct place of inclusion in our history and tradition. All of these activities engage the community in a further process of exploration and expression. By doing this, rather than narrowing the concept, we make it larger and hence easier to grasp.

A school I visited recently is situated in a very challenging community. Acknowledging the largely dysfunctional and often chaotic home life that most students experience, this secondary school chose the concept of 'family' as one of its values. If ever there was a concept that was increasingly hard to bring close definition to, it is surely this. Our contemporary notions of family life are rightly both hugely broad and vigorously contested. Hence, the staff chose to express the term by thickening it through multiple ways and means. One way they did this was by introducing compulsory lunches for all students and staff, a daily event they entitled 'The Family Meal.' Rejecting the fast-food, self-service canteen culture, the school hired an accomplished chef and now serve lunch to students and staff who sit together, serve one another, share basic chores and celebrate life as a school family every day. In addition, students learn to cook the highly nutritious menu and the school is about to open a restaurant to provide a similar experience for parents and the wider community. By thickening the value in these ways, the school has made it that much easier for staff and students to understand, own and express the value of 'family', regardless of their particular home life, culture or tradition. To this end, it has become far less likely that a student will choose to ignore or reject the value and, once again, far more likely that the value has a powerful transformative effect.

If organizations wish to help their members to understand the meaning and value of their values, then they should consider making those values 'thicker' and learning from the school above. By continually adding new layers of meaning, interpretation and application to specific values, and in so doing thickening the key ingredients, it becomes far easier and more likely, that community members will sign up to the scheme.

Conclusion

Before concluding this chapter it may help to retrace the ground covered so far. We have looked at three particular challenges to our understanding and implementation of values schemes. In responding to these challenges we have sought to identify opportunities to increase both the impact and efficacy of these initiatives.

First, we began by addressing the problem and importance of origination, where values schemes are concerned. Here we concluded that it is essential for a community to understand not only what their values are but where they came from, who ordained them and what it means to distil these principles in every aspect of school life.

Secondly, we looked at the challenge presented by overly pragmatic values schemes and noted that these often fail to provide a compelling enough vision for the educational task at hand. More than this we discovered that pragmatic values schemes all too easily reduce to a series of contractual procedures about how members of a community should behave. Pressing on, we suggested that a values scheme should move beyond rules and boundaries and provide a unique space in which students can develop character and learn virtues.

Thirdly, we raised the question of choice and addressed the challenge of how to communicate in such a way as to make it possible for a student to understand and appropriate a value. By resisting the tendency to narrow these terms and rather taking every opportunity to thicken the value through activities which lend more interpretation and greater meaning, educationalists can have a truly transformative effect on their students and their schools.

As is often the case in these chapters, it appears that we have spent the last pages frantically scratching the surface. That said, if we are prepared to keep talking and scratching, discussing and digging, who knows what we will discover or achieve in days to come? In recent years educationalists have become accustomed to measuring their impact by calculating the value that has been added to a student's learning and achievement in school. If nothing else, I hope that this discussion challenges those of us involved in education to reflect more deeply upon the greater values that we add to the lives of students, schools and communities. More so than any academic achievement or improvement, the first call of education is to add new layers of meaning, purpose, self-belief and aspiration to the lives of those we work with. By optimizing our values schemes we develop students, grow character, instil virtue, build confidence, heighten aspiration and generally make people bigger. In terms of values, we exist to make people thicker! Only when we have achieved this can we truly say that we have value added.

5 Changes in the school workforce

Patricia Collarbone

Context

Over the past ten years the number of schools funded by the government in England has fallen by around 1,200 and the number of full-time equivalent pupils in schools by in excess of 100,000. Over the same period revenue expenditure per pupil has increased by 76 per cent in real terms. The most dramatic statistical signal of this change is the numbers of full-time equivalent adults now employed in schools. In January 1997 there were just over a half million. By 2008 the figure was in excess of three quarters of a million with almost 200,000 of the increase being support staff. (all statistics DCSF)

While the statistics may be dramatic and perhaps to be expected with a rapid increase in funding throughout the first ten year years of this century, even more dramatic is the story behind the statistics. Throughout the 1980s and much of the 1990s, though support staff played an important role in the school, they were often treated badly with few opportunities for training and career development. Continuing Professional Development (CPD) was the preserve of teachers and the limited training support staff received was frequently as a direct result of gaps in organizational provision rather than motivated by the development needs of the individual.

The introduction of Local Management of Schools (LMS) and Grant Maintained (GM) schools in 1990 began to change that, particularly for administration staff and, to a lesser extent, premises staff. The standards agenda and particularly the literacy and numeracy policies brought about the realization that teaching assistants were a valuable but under-used resource in schools and by the turn of the century the necessary training and development opportunities were beginning to be in place.

A changing mood at government, employer and union level was, within two years, to totally change the roles of teachers and support staff and heralded new ways of working in schools forever. The need for radical change had first been posted in the Green Paper published in 1998, *Teachers: Meeting the Challenge of Change*. But this had been targeted at teachers, almost as if support staff did not exist. It promised new professional development opportunities, a new performance management system, better leadership and the National College for School Leadership (NCSL). The promises made were generally kept but fundamentally the basic issue was not even addressed as the PricewaterhouseCoopers report of 2001 was to reveal. Teachers and school leaders were overworked and many of them were not always focused on learning and teaching. Something needed to be done, as far as the government was concerned, particularly if standards were to continue to rise in the coming years.

Levers to inject real change and open up flexibility in schools were about to be positioned. By the end of 2002 we had the Education Act 2002 with its provocative Section 133 and the publication of *Time for Standards: Reforming the School Workforce*. The implications of the importance of this latter document and the accompanying consultation documents should not be underestimated when trying to understand why England now leads the world in school workforce reform. On 15 January 2003 the majority of the teacher unions, the support staff unions, the Employers' Organisation, the DfES and the Welsh Assembly signed a historic agreement and the workforce in schools would never be the same again.

The school workforce today

Generally speaking the school workforce today is a very different animal than it was at the turn of the century. The Training and Development Agency for Schools (TDA) identifies five areas where support staff not only play key roles but also are required to play leadership roles.

- Learning support, including Higher Level Teaching Assistants (HLTAs), which may well require preparing lessons and delivering those lessons to whole classes.
- Administrative roles, including School Business Managers (SBMs) who are often members of the Senior Leadership Teams (SLT), exam officers and timetablers.
- Pupil support, which includes a range of roles including learning managers, which, in some cases have replaced teacher Heads of Year, learning mentors, a result of the Excellence in City programmes, and pupil services managers.
- Specialist and technical staff. These are not necessarily new roles, although there has been a major increase in ICT technicians. There has also been a growth in the use of learning resource managers and professionally trained librarians.
- Site staff. Again not a new area but an area that is changing, particularly as the extended services agenda develops. For example, the site manager becomes a key leadership figure in how the school is run. This is an area likely to develop dramatically over the next 20 years. Another major area of focus in recent years is the healthy food initiative, which has real implications for the development of any on-site dinner team.

The key role for schools, as a result of the publication of Every Child Matters in 2003, is extended services. As of March 2009 74 per cent of schools in England are delivering access to the full core offer including 68 per cent of rural schools (the most challenging area), well ahead of government targets. Part of this is the direct result of the appointment of extended schools coordinators or cluster managers and the introduction of Parent Support Advisers (PSAs). Neither of these roles should be held by teachers and the concept of teachers holding all the key roles in schools is rapidly becoming an issue of the past.

The massive investment in school capital programmes over the next 15 years, i.e. Building Schools for the Future and the Primary Schools Capital programme suggests that the future of schooling is secured, at least for the next 50 years, but that does not mean that current practices are preserved. The focus has changed and the advent of personalization has created new challenges for almost all schools. In fact it is my belief that over the next few years schools will cease to be perceived as traditional institutions of a state-dominated education system and will be replaced by learning organizations and social centres with the learning and social development needs of children, young people and their families at the centre of their work.

The publication of *The Children's Plan: Building Brighter Futures* in December 2007 reinforces this vision and supports the existing agenda for change. The workforce action plan *Brighter Futures: Next Steps for the Children's Workforce* (2008a) sets out an agenda for the children's workforce which means up-skilling, personalization and partnership working right across all sectors. The Children's Trust in each authority is going to play the key strategic role, if it is not already doing so. Schools will be at the hub of their communities and their very survival may depend on this. Good, deliberately designed examples are the Chafford Hundred Campus in Thurrock and the multi-agency Hadley Learning Community in Telford and Wrekin. There are also hundreds of examples where schools have adapted for wider community use in more traditional school settings.

2020 Children and Young People's Workforce Strategy (December 2008) set out a more specific agenda for the school's workforce with its commitments to:

- Encourage clusters of schools to work together to deliver CPD – this is aimed to help effectiveness and efficiency.
- Establish a CPD entitlement for every teacher linked to the performance management framework – currently the DCSF are in discussions with the social partnership and the TDA on what this might mean.
- Support continuing improvement in performance – for all teachers, support staff and headteachers.
- Make teaching a Masters-level profession – the Masters in Teaching and Learning (MTL) will be available to Newly Qualified Teachers (NQTs) in the North West and in National Challenge schools.
- Ensure the succession of high quality leadership in schools – many school leaders are due to retire within the next six years and the NCSL is working with others to develop more effective succession planning.

- Develop a new generation of business managers – schools are much more complex organizations today and need the knowledge and skills of professionals able to secure value for money while allowing the teacher members of the senior leadership team to focus on learning and teaching.
- Establish a School Support Staff Negotiating Body – this group started work in September 2008.
- Develop a more systematic approach to professional development for support staff – the TDA is working hard on this and has developed national standards for HLTAs, and national occupational standards for those supporting teaching and learning as well as other support staff. By 2010 there will be an Integrated Qualification Framework (IQF) for all those working with children and young people.

Leading and managing change

This agenda is about change and change not experienced on this scale before. In order to implement the agenda required to make the dream of 'a world class education' system in place by 2020 requires a cultural change on the part of schools, other children services and local authorities. The children's agenda is focused on five particular areas over the next phase of the spending review (which lasts until March 2011).

- Raise the educational achievement of all children and young people. This is the long-standing standards agenda but the targets for 2020 require 80 per cent achieving Level 2 qualifications (5+ GCSE A*–C grades or equivalent but now including English and maths) and 70 per cent achieving Level 3 qualifications (A Level or equivalent). By 2015 all young people will be required to be participating in education or training till age 18, so this will present a new challenge to local authorities, schools and FE Colleges to build the capacity necessary.
- Narrow the gap in educational achievement between children from low-income and disadvantaged backgrounds and their peers. This has been an identified area for schools for a number of years and improvements have happened. However, despite the extra expenditure in 2007, 21.1 per cent of young people entitled to free school meals achieved 5+ A*–C (including English and maths) compared to 49.1 per cent of young people who were not entitled.
- Improve the health and well-being of children and young people. The healthy schools initiative and the new nutritional standards for school food are among a range of measures intended to improve the health of children and young people. Since September 2007 governing bodies of schools have been charged with the legal duty to promote well-being as defined by the Children Act 2004.
- Improve children and young people's safety. Today anyone who is working with children and young people in a school, including governors and those providing extended services, must undergo a Criminal Records Bureau check to ensure they are fit to work with their charges. Security has increased in schools in recent years and health and safety rules are now much tighter.

- Increase the number of children and young people on the path to success. There are a number of requirements on schools to help children and young people make a positive contribution and achieve economic well-being, the two Every Child Matters outcomes most associated with this Public Service Agreement. Requirements include promotion of the pupil voice, the changing curriculum, extended services and personalized learning.

The changing responsibilities on schools demand a different style of leadership. Research conducted by the University of Manchester for NCSL concluded:

- The research literature currently available provides only a partial account of developments on the ground
- Changes in local arrangements are helping schools to cope with an increasingly complex education agenda
- The local context plays an important role in the adoption and development of new leadership patterns and structures
- Innovative and traditional approaches appear in combination
- New leadership arrangements that are seen as liberating by some staff can be seen to increase constraints and pressures felt by others
- The picture is fluid and the pace of change rapid (Chapman et al, 2007)

These findings led the researchers to conclude that there are signs of a movement towards a more co-ordinated and systematic approach to education provision and there are significant changes in leadership and management roles and the responsibilities of those working in schools.

Collarbone, in her recent publication *Creating Tomorrow: Planning, Developing and Sustaining Change in Education and Other Public Services* (2009) argues:

> the new – remodelled – role of leaders is to enable others to come up with ideas. Leadership becomes fully focused on empowering the whole workforce, on capitalizing on all the skills and creativity it holds. In this technological age, where knowledge management and intellectual capital are the prime currency, this is key to ongoing organizational success. (page 92)

Meanwhile in their *Independent Study into School Leadership* (2007) for the DfES, PricewaterhouseCoopers suggested:

> There is a clear sense among school leaders that their role has become more challenging, and that the complexity and range of tasks they are required to undertake has increased greatly in recent years. This is due in large part to a number of inter-related policies and initiatives that impact on the role of school leaders including Every Child Matters (ECM), workforce remodelling, and the 14–19 agenda. Implementation of these initiatives requires a new set of skills including greater collaboration between schools, and partnership working across the children's services sector and beyond. (page v)

Research evidence points to the complexity the modern headteacher and other school leaders face as they go about their day to day work. This is leading to new models of leadership among headteachers including co-headship, executive headteachers and heads of federations. But changes to leadership responsibilities in schools is not restricted to headteachers. The introduction of teaching and learning responsibility (TLRs) awards to replace management allowances in 2005 have a clear emphasis on leadership. The School Teachers' Pay and Conditions Document requires deputy and assistant headteachers to play a major role under the overall direction of the head teacher in:

a   Formulating the aims and objectives of the school
b   Establishing the policies through which they are to be achieved
c   Managing staff and resources to that end
d   Monitoring progress towards their achievement; (DCSF, 2008b; para 65.2, page 123)

The national standards for school teachers require leadership roles for those teachers that have crossed the threshold and particularly for Excellent Teachers and Advanced Skills Teachers. Nor is leadership in schools limited to teachers. The introduction of HLTAs and the growth in the numbers of SBMs are just two examples of new leadership roles for support staff. Extended services in schools has also created new leadership roles for support staff and others from beyond the traditional school workforce.

For all school leaders the emphasis these days is on leading and managing change. In his 2001 publication Michael Fullan describes the need for leadership that achieves and includes:

- A moral purpose
- Understanding change
- Relationship building
- Knowledge creation and sharing
- Coherence making

It requires building trust, redesigning jobs, changing organizational structures and developing learning cultures. But in order to achieve these aims school leaders need to carry followers with them. And in order to achieve this it requires shared leadership and an acceptance that the best leaders are those that facilitate followers to believe that they did it themselves (to paraphrase Lao-Tzu).

Collarbone and West-Burnham (2008) have suggested that a major developmental route for school leaders is systems leadership, a concept they accept is difficult to define. However they have developed a typology of different ways in which school leaders can impact the education system.

1   School leadership – focus on school improvement.
2   Leadership of extended services – changing responsibility in terms of time, resources, space and activity.

3　Executive leadership – direct involvement in the leadership of a second or third school.

4　Leading networks, clusters and federations – varying degrees of responsibility and authority over the work of other schools.

5　Leading community initiatives – active partnership and involvement across community initiatives.

6　Working for local authorities – advisory work, consultant leaders, school improvement partners, guidance on policy.

7　Collaborating with other agencies – working in the context of the Children Act

8　Advising on national policies and strategies – direct involvement with DCFS through associations, think tanks and/or advisory bodies.

Change process

In order to develop the change agenda necessary requires a change process that leads people through the changes that are taking place and takes them with those leading the way through the agenda. Nobody finds change easy – it disrupts the order within which they live.

There are many change processes available to schools including one developed by John Kotter (1996). Kotter advocates that it is important to:

• Establish a sense of urgency
• Create the guiding coalition
• Develop a vision and strategy
• Communicate the change vision
• Empower broad-based action
• Generate short-term wins
• Consolidate gains and produce more change
• Anchor new approaches in the culture

The Kotter principles have been incorporated into the remodelling process developed for schools. The remodelling process is now owned by the TDA but was originally developed by the National Remodelling Team (NRT). The NRT was created at the behest of the social partnership (a partnership consisting of the Department, the Welsh Assembly, the National Employers' Organisation for School Teachers (NEOST) and the school trade unions/professional associations), the signatories to the national agreement. The NRT was a partnership between education and change consultants from the business world. Remodelling has been used officially to develop implementation of the national agreement, targeted youth support, financial management in schools and the extended schools agenda. As an offshoot of the extended schools agenda it was key in developing the School Improvement Planning Framework and the PSA programme. It continues to be used in schools to deal with a diverse range of issues such as curriculum change, capital build and lunchtime arrangements.

The remodelling process involves looking collaboratively at particular issues and coming up with individual local solutions – one size doesn't fit all. It enables individual schools to produce plans, actions and outcomes that are made to measure. To be fully effective it should include six core elements:

- Effective leadership
- Inclusive culture
- Constructive collaboration
- Proactive change team
- Proven change process
- Rational, political and emotional considerations.

Next steps

In December 2008 the DCSF published *21st Century Schools: A World-Class Education for Every Child*. This publication expands the vision for schools in England in the twenty-first century and increases the pressure for even greater change and at a faster rate than has been hitherto achieved.

> schools work more extensively and effectively with parents, other providers and wider children's services. (DCSF, 2008c: page 7)

The expectation is that such partnership working will improve outcomes for all children and young people and ultimately improve their future life chances. The set of demands is not in itself new:

- Providing a more personalized approach for each child and young person, through ensuring greater integrated working and coherence between services (across all services).
- Delivering a wider offer: schools can provide collectively, and with other partners, a greater range of provision than they can alone (extended services, 14–19 agenda).
- Meeting additional needs: as the main universal children's service, schools are key to ensuring problems are identified early and addressed (swift and easy access to targeted services).
- Contributing to school improvement through maximizing the impact of the best leaders and governors and sharing effective practice and professional development (greater use of hard and soft federations and cluster arrangements).
- Making the best use of resources: for example, through sharing staff, functions and facilities across a number of school sites (even more collaboration).
- Ensuring greater collective accountability for outcomes for children and young people in the local area (through, for example, extending the role of the Children's Trust and extending the number of 'relevant partners' under a duty to cooperate to include all schools, sixth form and FE colleges and Job Centre Plus). (DCSF, 2008c: pages 7–8)

The implications for the workforce are dramatic and the training and development needs extensive. The key agencies responsible for training and development, the TDA (school workforce), NCSL (school leaders) and the Children's Workforce Development Council (CWDC) (many of the others who work within children's services) have developed working protocols to enable them to work more closely together. The three agencies are committed to collaboration nationally and regionally to ensure a more effective use of resources to meet the specific needs of organizations delivering services in local areas.

The Integrated Qualifications Framework (IQF) – a set of approved qualifications that allows progression, continuing professional development and mobility across the children and young people's workforce – is currently under development through a partnership led by the CWDC on behalf of the Children's Workforce Network (a strategic partnership of 12 national agencies and other partners including GTC, NCSL and TDA). Currently under evaluation to ensure it is fit for purpose, the IQF is due to go live in 2010.

National standards exist for teachers at all stages of their careers, for headteachers, for HLTAs and for others who support teaching and learning as well as other support staff. These are all subject to revision as needs change. National standards are designed to support the direction of professional development and training needs, provide direction for performance reviews, aid career development and assist with school improvement planning.

Training and development and the use of national standards are not the only challenges posed by the developing role of the twenty-first century school. Workforce modernization remains a continuing priority for all schools. While major changes have already taken place in many schools and teachers are generally more focused on teaching and learning, over the next two years there are likely to be major changes in the pay and conditions of service of many of the school's support staff. A continuing issue is the unrelenting workload of school leaders and, while the National Agreement did attempt to address such issues, there remains ample evidence that school leaders, and particularly headteachers, continue to overwork. Increasing expectations from stakeholders, particularly parents/carers and their children will place new pressures and demands on schools. The expansion of pupil rights and the pupil voice, though laudable on both moral and outcome levels, produces its own challenges and for many schools this remains an issue that still needs addressing. Interagency working requires a new culture and new levels of trust and while this is developing there remains some way to go before all schools will be truly providing a world-class children's and young people's service.

Conclusion

In 1997 I launched the London Leadership Centre at the Institute of Education, University of London. Since that time schools, their staff and school leadership have undergone a more dramatic change than I ever witnessed as a school teacher and headteacher in almost 30 years of working in schools.

The election of a Labour government that year with its priority on education may well have been the catalyst for such a degree of change and they certainly have made it possible through the increase in expenditure on education and a myriad of demands on schools. This chapter has already set out what many of those changes have meant for schools.

Initially, however, expenditure did not increase yet the pressures did. By the turn of the century the situation did begin to change. The development of the social partnership has played its part in how the agenda has developed. Another key lever was the publication of the Every Child Matters Green Paper in 2003 in response to Lord Laming's inquiry into the death of Victoria Climbié.

It is also important to recognize the strong support for the agenda provided by many schools and particularly their leaders who have made it possible. The support from many local authorities is impressive and shows they can be trusted with the agenda. Government regional offices are now well involved in the DCSF agenda, as are the government agencies charged with delivery. They are there to support but have now been charged with a greater sense of urgency. The world is not slowing down.

6 Gateway: the ownership of education by communities

Max Coates

It is unlikely that you will remember 25 November 2004. This was the date of the first of four planned strikes by teaching assistants in Brighton and Hove. At the time it was widely reported by the media. The significance of the day was the impact of the strike, which resulted in some 30 schools being closed. Ten years previously the strike would probably have gone unnoticed outside the local press and the schools would have remained open as usual.

Parents have been allowed into schools for many years to help with reading, swimming or perhaps to make up adult numbers on school trips and outings. In less PC days they were often referred to as the 'mummy army'. In fact they were hugely valued by many heads and pragmatically endured by others. This involvement of adults in schools tended to be more prevalent in the primary phase where children were prepared to admit to having parents. In secondary schools such adults were relatively rare as the reduced dependency of the older children allowed parents the opportunity to return to work. Of course many teenagers find parents terminally embarrassing and would prefer to be the products of a clandestine cloning experiment. They certainly would not welcome parental presence anywhere near their school. Arguably, it was the Warnock watershed that triggered significant change. This report in 1978 brought pupils with special needs centre stage. It was suggested that schools would have around 20 per cent of pupils in this category. Significant numbers of pupils now had their needs identified and increased support allocated. The support assistant drawn significantly from the ranks of women returners became increasingly commonplace. The bar was raised again when, in January 2003, the government launched a National Agreement for England and Wales on 'Raising Standards and Tackling Workload'. In September 2005 this legislation started to bite with teachers having an entitlement to planning and preparation time. Gaps and tasks were filled by a rising tide of para-teachers.

Schools are now routinely staffed by a mixed economy of qualified teachers and 'others'. The latter have burgeoned into Teaching Assistants, Higher Level Teaching Assistants, Learning Support Assistants, Cover Supervisors and Learning Mentors. Many of course are still these same women returners who have completed an intensive course in child development as parents. However increasing numbers of such assistants are not derived from this predominantly female labour pool. The roles have become established in their own right in the same way that Health Care Assistants have become embedded in the health service. Entering the educational shop floor has required not merely skills, but also qualifications and certification. Initially these were pragmatic, dealing with issues such as Criminal Records Bureau (CRB) and areas such as manual handling and lifting. This impromptu workforce was in many instances comprised of highly educated individuals with skills derived from other careers. Some ten years ago I employed a lady who had previously been a social worker. It would have been inappropriate, and indeed impossible, for her to lay down those extensive and higher level skills because she was employed in a different context. In a life long learning culture it is both appropriate and inevitable that a qualification and accreditation structure would follow.

In the 1990s through to the present two acts of 'badge engineering' took place. Most secondary schools were designated by a specialism (though to date nobody has developed a 'Learning College') and the other was to add the epithet 'community'. In some cases the latter was a fitting summary of existing work, while in other schools the title hung rather awkwardly on the headed notepaper. Community education has rich roots. The following is taken from a 1942 BBC broadcast by Henry Morris, the creator of the Cambridgeshire Village College:

> [The school] is designed so that all its workshops and laboratories can be used by both adults and adolescents. You may go there any evening and find hundreds of young people and parents enjoying a general programme of lectures, crafts, games, dance, cinema, or simply sitting in the common room over a cup of coffee and a magazine. The school here is not isolated but part of a community pattern.

Morris' work was largely a response to revitalize rural communities. Our current endeavours to increase the permeability between the school and its embedded community are more probably political and philosophical in origin.

Post-modernism has stripped schools and hospitals of their previous magical status. A wider community now feels a drive to engage and own such enterprises. More recently the emergence of the extended schools movement presents a fascinating paradox. On the one hand it stands squarely within the frame of extending the use of the schools to resource their communities, while on the other it remains largely a movement of service provision. Its core purpose is the provision of a child-minding service to support women participating more fully in the workforce and a base for co-located services for Every Child Matters; to support parents and impact upon anti-social behaviour that arises from deficiencies in parenting; and to give children in maintained schools the rich extra-curricular opportunities available in independent schools. All these are a response to contemporary needs. They are, however, different from integrated community education – community development. They remain an apposite development but are rooted in provision rather than local ownership. It has ultimately driven schools to commission, host or signpost activities rather than manage them.

There remains a nascent drive by communities to shape and engage with locally delivered services. However, in many areas the delivery of these services stops with lighting-up times as the professionals retreat from the community to their homes, often many miles away. In most schools it is the HLTAs and TAs who remain present 24/7 in the geographical context of the school. Increasingly they are becoming an important, though an often ill-managed, interface between the school and its community. The significance of these para-educators is being routinely underestimated, as will be the next wave of community incursion through community practitioners. This latter group are amorphous and ill-defined. Experience through the Innovation Unit's 'Communities for Learning' initiative (2008–2009) has shown some are enthusiasts seeking a platform within schools, while others are derived from schools seeking out skills and resources within their communities.

There is a vast wealth of human resource within our communities often available as a consequence of extended healthy retirement or flexible working hours. In many cases these hugely gifted individuals need 'child friendly' pedagogical skills honing. The emerging question is where will such pedagogical expertise be sourced? Certainly some providers from within traditional schooling have stepped up to the bar. Increasingly, however, there is a search for alternative approaches which are more in tune with the practitioners' own *weltanschauung* or world view. The way they work does not fit into a campanologically defined timeframe or nationally defined curriculum which is inherently economically focused. These practitioners are alive with life skills, views about sustainability, the nature of community and, increasingly, with views about the nature of pedagogy itself.

Pedagogy for community empowerment

> For many educators the concept of learning is implicit and assumed. In some usages it implies what the learners does in response to teaching: 'If you don't pay attention to me you won't learn this.' A common usage equates learning with memorization: 'I want you to learn this for a test tomorrow.' The paucity of our understanding of learning is often reflected in the lack of any shared or common agreement between teachers, let alone learners, as to what the process actually involves. Although the situation is now changing, many schools do not have a shared vocabulary as to what constitutes learning – it is usually judged as a product rather than a process – 'I have learned this.' What 'learning this' actually involves is elusive and not codified. There is little doubt that this is, to a significant extent, the result of a curriculum that is focused on information transfer and the means of assessment that value the 'correct' answer. Most national schooling systems focus on this narrow, instrumental and reductionist view of learning and this is reinforced by prevailing models of accountability, which value outcomes that allow for generic compatibility rather than individual capability.
> (West-Burnham and Coates, 2005: page 34)

Education has a significant socio-economic function and is often the means whereby the members of society are inducted into its norms of the same. The prevailing model in the UK is the transmission of knowledge by professionals in purpose-built institutions. It is not always surprising that such an imposed process engenders resistance as its message often confirms disadvantaged communities in their failure and disempowerment. Such a model has many similarities with vaccination but often takes less well.

The current conceptualization of education normally starts with the content of the curriculum. Seldom are the implications of the pedagogy given adequate consideration.

It is almost hackneyed but the African proverb 'It takes a village to raise a child' still has much underlying wisdom. What if community wisdom was encouraged and localized endeavour was nurtured through the development of a coaching pedagogy that progressively levers community participation in education? In supporting such empowerment, achievement, aspiration and hope would also be generated.

The school improvement model is ultimately about a specific school conforming to an abstract norm of performance derived from the results of other schools and central government intent. Consider for a moment that the actual performance of a school or locality was analyzed and served as the floor below which learning was not allowed to fall. Arguably this would free the school and community to generate alternative strategies. Clearly it would be hoped that other key performance indicators would be employed, set against the Every Child Matters agenda which has a community-wide perspective. An unfortunate outcome of the tragedy of Baby Peter in Haringey is that the well-being of the many has been obscured by the singular.

The focus of transformation could be based upon a school with a 'change team'. This would consist of a multi-disciplinary team with a teaching team with an excess of 25–30 per cent over complement. The contractual commitment would be for three years and could well bring retired or semi-retired teachers and other professionals into the mix. The teaching workforce would be trained in mentoring and coaching with a mandate to teach and also develop members of the local community as TAs and HLTAs. The teaching team would in turn be linked to a representative of an Higher Education Institution with a frontline support role and also engaged in direct support for local community members to develop as teachers. The programme would be self-consciously about short-term support and, in the long term, withdrawal of the change team.

Additionally other members of the community would be included in developing sustainability projects and they in turn would be backed by support and opportunities to gain qualifications.

Many of these communities have either low aspiration, low levels of hope or, indeed, a combination of the two. In turn such beliefs are modelled by the adults and thus transmitted to their children. The manifestations of such belief systems are ultimately a range of dysfunctional behaviours.

The pedagogical model is clearly focused on mentoring and coaching. The former to address barriers to learning and motivation, the latter to generate skills. Such a pedagogy is quite distinct from tutoring. Its outcomes transcend any other current pedagogical approach. Consider the work of Joyce and Showers (1988):

- 5 per cent of learners will transfer a new skill into their practice as a result of theory
- 10 per cent of learners will transfer a new skill into their practice as a result of theory and demonstration
- 20 per cent of learners will transfer a new skill into their practice as a result of theory, demonstration and practice
- 25 per cent of learners will transfer a new skill into their practice as a result of theory, demonstration, practice and feedback
- 90 per cent of learners will transfer a new skill into their practice as a result of theory, demonstration, practice, feedback and coaching

If telling people was all it takes to educate the task of teaching would be an easy one. The reality is that education is a complex process, which is appropriately supported by this approach. The argument is that, not only will learning be enhanced, but also that barriers to learning will be dismantled. The intention would be to establish a tipping point of people who work in this way which, in turn, will transform community interaction and function. This has never been undertaken before largely because with disadvantaged community the interventions are often directive, invasive and prescriptive.

As schools become more permeable to their communities and engage with individuals who are dancing to a different educational drumbeat a tension will develop. Issues around pedagogy will be high on the explicit or implicit agenda. It could of course develop a synergy but, conversely, an uncomfortable challenge to existing practice could result.

There is the potential for collision between these para-teachers and their community practitioner cousins with designated educational professionals. If the received wisdom on pedagogy is that teachers are more engaged with content than with learning methodology then they will find it difficult to mount a robust defence of current practice. Contemporary pedagogy is a castle without walls. Some of these interactions will be constructive, some tense, some strategic and some unintended. There will be conflict between those who are deriving a new pedagogy but lack clear definition of their role or status. Potentially there will be a change from the school engaging with its community to the school becoming a community resource for life-long learning where the locus of power will move from the qualified professional to the empowered resident. The change may well be subversive; it will certainly be pervasive.

Part 2
THE EVOLVING SCHOOL

7 From schooling to learning

John West-Burnham

Introduction

This discussion is based on seven core propositions that will hopefully help to explore the tension between models of schooling and models of effective learning. At the outset it is important to stress that one of the key issues in this debate is the problematic status of learning. Schools often see learning as the positive response by learners to the teaching of the curriculum – therefore learning is often described in terms of social behaviour rather than a cognitive process – 'if you do not settle down you will not learn anything'. In fact everybody is learning all the time. The seven propositions together comprise a challenge to many prevailing orthodoxies about the nature, purpose and organization of schooling:

- Every learner is unique
- Learning is a neurological function
- Learning is a social process
- Intelligence can be learnt
- Understanding is the key criterion for effective learning
- Communities can learn
- Learning can take place anytime, anywhere with anyone

Every learner is unique

According to Leadbeater (2004):

> we need a new framework to show how personal needs can be taken into account within universal equity and excellence in education. . . we can only understand these terms by putting the needs and wants of individual learners at the heart of the system. (page 6)

This reflects a social, moral and political stance, but it is also a position based in scientific evidence:

> Possessing different kinds of minds, individuals represent information and knowledge in different ways. (Gardner, 1999: page 245)

It is the combination of the moral and the scientific perspectives that points to the need for a radical reappraisal of the role and status of the individual learner. Morally there is the need to design educational experiences that start from the premise of the value and dignity of the person. Education in a modern, liberal democracy has to be rooted in the premise of the entitlement to learning on the person's own terms. The movement from schooling to educating is very much the process of starting with the individual and designing learning experiences on their terms rather than having to comply with, and respond to, generic experiences which may, or may not, be appropriate

Learning is a neurological function

There is probably not a science of learning at present. There is no definitive or authoritative synthesis available of the wide range of scientific research that may impinge on our understanding of the learning process. Research in genetics, neurological functioning and cognitive psychology does seem to point to the possibility of increased empirical knowledge about how we learn. However, it would be premature to claim that there is a holistic theory of learning in the offing. It is equally important to view with caution claims made on the basis of research, which was never intended to inform learning and teaching in schools. And then there are the panaceas promoted on the basis of limited scientific research but with no claim to universifiability – open access to water, Omega-3 supplements, brain gym and playing Mozart are not harmful; they *may* indeed be helpful, but they are not based in scientific research.

Hard scientific data about learning is very elusive but there are significant developments which may lead to profound changes in the conceptual framework that informs our thinking about the nature of learning. Educational theory and practice have been dominated very largely by a view of the world that according to Pinker:

> divides matter from mind, the material from the spiritual, the physical from the mental, biology from culture, nature from society, and science from the social sciences. (Pinker, 2002: page 31)

Not surprisingly, educationalists have believed, and created an education system around the belief that the schooling process is the means by which the tabula rasa or blank slate is filled. As Pinker caricatures it 'children come to school empty and have knowledge deposited in them' (2002: page 222). For Pinker:

> Education is neither writing on a blank slate nor allowing the child's nobility to come into flower. Rather education is a technology that tries to make up for what the human mind is innately bad at. (ibid)

Our genetic and evolutionary inheritance means that we have a predisposition to speak; we do not have such a predisposition to write or to read. Education is a process of compensating for gaps in our biological inheritance and adapting natural predispositions 'to master problems for which they were not designed' (page 223).

> And this offers priorities for educational policy: to provide students with the cognitive tools that are most important for grasping the modern world and that are most unlike the cognitive tools they are born with. (ibid: page 235)

This is an argument for both a better understanding of the impact of our genetic inheritance and recognition that the blank slate and genetic determinism arguments are both wrong. Ridley (2003) argues:

> Nature versus nurture is dead. Long live nature via nurture. (page 280)

Our capacity to learn is the result of complex interactions at the most fundamental level of what makes us human. The most powerful expression of this interaction is our neurological functioning. The brain is the most powerful example of the interaction between our genetic make-up and the environment in which we live. The starting point for this discussion has to be a very simple but highly contentious proposition – learning is a physical process. There is no 'ghost in the machine'.

> So everything we think and feel can ultimately be boiled down to this alternating sequence of electrical and chemical events. The electrical signal arriving along the axon is converted into a chemical signal that carries it across the physical barrier, the synapse, between the neurons. (Greenfield, 2000: page 39)

Our capacity to learn is the result of an incredibly complex equation of which neural processing is only a part. Gardner (1999: page 81) identifies for educators seven implications for educators arising out of brain and mind research:

1 The tremendous importance of early experience
2 The imperative 'use it or lose it'
3 The flexibility of the early nervous system
4 The importance of action and activity
5 The specificity of human abilities and talents
6 The possible organizing role played in early childhood by music
7 The crucial role played by emotional coding

Learning is a social process

The increasing recognition of the importance of emotional intelligence in all aspects of human collaboration is rooted firmly in neurological science. The core proposition is very simple – our emotional responses to the world are so powerful that they can overwhelm most cognitive processes. For Greenfield (2000):

> The question of emotions is one of the most important that a brain scientist, or indeed anyone, can explore. We are guided and controlled by our emotions. They shape our lives as we attempt to maximise some, such as happiness, and obliterate others, such as fear. (page 107)

Simplistic thinking in this area sees the brain as a battleground between the emotions and reason, between EQ and IQ. Inevitably, the picture is much more complicated in that our behaviour, and therefore our capacity to learn, is the result of a complex series of permutations and interactions in the brain, which are, in turn, the result of our learnt experiences.

> This tight orchestration of thought and feeling is made possible by what amounts to a superhighway in the brain, a bundle of neurons connecting the prefrontal lobes, behind the forehead – the brain's executive decision-making center – with an area deep in the brain that harbors our emotions. (Goleman, 1998: page 24)

As our understanding of this relationship grows, so do the implications for the management of the learning process and Pinker (2002: page 40) argues that it is possible to identify three interacting components of the brain:

- First, it has distinct interaction processing systems for 'learning skills, controlling the body, remembering facts, holding information temporarily, and storing and executing rules.'
- Secondly, there are mental faculties 'dedicated to different kinds of content, such as language, number, space, tools and living things.'
- Thirdly, there are the systems for motivation and emotion, the 'affect programs.'

Pinker concludes:

> Behaviour is not just elicited or emitted, nor does it come directly out of culture or society. It comes from an internal struggle among mental modules with differing agendas and goals. (ibid)

From this perspective, brain functioning, and therefore learning, can be seen as a complex interplay between information processing, mental faculties and the affect programs. These factors, what Pinker calls 'combinatorial software' are the essence of our capacity to learn and to use that learning. Our knowledge of these three elements is limited; even more uncertain is how they interact and how the multiple permutations they offer might be better understood and managed. What is clear, and available, is the potential to develop and enhance each of these elements and so enrich their 'combinatorial' capacity. From this perspective learning is essentially relational – it is only in social interaction that the full potential of learning is likely to be realized. This means that the social organization of learning (e.g. schools) need to be designed to optimize highly effective social relationships.

Intelligence can be learnt

The debate around the nature of intelligence is central to any view of learning in the future. Most education systems are still dominated by four fundamental assumptions about intelligence:

- Intelligence is expressed through logical and reasoning abilities
- These abilities can be measured quantitatively
- Such measures are predictive
- Intelligence is fixed for life

These assumptions form the design principles of many school systems and determine the professional practice in many classrooms. For example, they can be used to justify selection at age 11, banding, streaming and setting and the divorce of academic and vocational work. This view of intelligence also explains strategies for assessment, the nature of the curriculum, models of accountability and dominant modes of teaching. A key influence in the development of this view in Britain was Cyril Burt who argued that intelligence was 80 per cent genetic in origin – which might explain the confidence in predestination implicit to many education systems. Burt also argued 'once a defective, always a defective' (Overy, 2009: page 137) and he believed that:

> However much we educated the ignorant, trained the imbecile, cured the lunatic, and reformed the criminal, their offspring would inherit, not the results of education, but the original ignorance, not the acquired training but the original imbecility; not the acquired sanity, but the original predisposition to lunacy; not the moral reform, but the original tendency to crime. (Overy, 2009: page 110)

This is a deeply pessimistic view of human nature and is profoundly misconceived – not only is it morally repugnant, it is scientifically wrong. Ridley (2003) reviewing studies of twins found that:

> IQ is approximately 50 per cent 'additively genetic', 25 per cent influenced by the shared environment and 25 per cent influenced by factors unique to the individual. (page 90)

Ridley points to two other crucial findings: firstly, living in poverty has a profound impact on IQ – environment outweighs genetics. Secondly, ageing reduces the effect of family environment on IQ and genetic factors become more significant. If these points are accepted then many of the fundamental assumptions underpinning schooling are called into question. Schooling fails to come to terms with environmental issues and what we are learning about the influence of genetics. The essential model of schooling is a reflection of theoretical assumptions and if these change then the model of schooling has to change. To build an educational system around IQ, which is so culturally and chronologically specific, is to deny the full human potential of an individual.

I view giftedness as being of multiple kinds, as would be retardation. Componential, experimental and contextual strengths and weaknesses can all lead to different patterns of giftedness or retardation, and hence, for me, giftedness and retardation are in no way unitary phenomena. (Sternberg, 1990: page 299)

Sternberg's view has, of course, much in common with Gardner's view of multiple intelligences; both offer a response to the potentially inhibiting model based around IQ. If our understanding of intelligence moves from a unitary to a federal model then a range of assumptions about the nature of the curriculum, the nature of schooling, the role of the teacher, the patterns of assessment and accreditation are all called into question.

The response to this challenge lies in what Gardner characterizes as 'literacy skills, disciplinary skills and the possibility of multidisciplinary or interdisciplinary approaches' (ibid). A further challenge to the historical model of intelligence is the recognition that intelligence is, partly, a social construct based on interactions.

I want to capture the important fact that intelligence, which comes to life during human activities, may be crafted. There are both social and material dimensions of this distribution. (Pea, 1993: page 50)

Intelligence is a construct; socially through relationships and interactions, and materially in response to the environment and artefacts. Intelligence is dynamic and fluid. In fact, intelligence can be learnt and can be taught.

Understanding is the most important criterion for assessing learning

One of the great challenges facing schools and those who work in them is to develop a shared understanding of the learning process. All too often learning is described in social or passive terms rather than in any engagement with higher order cognitive activity. Perkins (1992) offers a model of effective learning that is based on the ability of the learner to demonstrate understanding rather than simply be able to replicate information. Understanding is about the creation of knowledge:

So let us view understanding not as a state of possession but one of enablement. When we understand about something, we not only possess certain information about it but are enabled to do certain things with that knowledge. (Perkins, 1992: page 77)

Perkins goes on to offer criteria by which to judge the extent to which understanding has been achieved

- Explanation
- Exemplification
- Transfer

- Justification
- Comparison
- Contextualization
- Generalization

In many ways this list offers, in microcosm, the cognitive strategies and skills that are fundamental to effective learning. In many schools these are the focus of a wide range of learning experiences. Unfortunately they do not always feature in the assessment strategies of the schooling system which tends to prefer measurement of information retention rather than understanding – even though it is the latter that actually makes a difference to people's lives.

Communities can learn to learn

Schools, owing much of their design to the factory system, tend to work as hierarchical organizations. Schooling tends to formalize and institutionalize learning; ignoring what has been known throughout human history, that 'it takes a village to raise a child'.

However much a cliché this is, it is a cliché because it is true. Schooling can be seen as arbitrary and artificial because it denies two fundamental truths – children spend about 15 per cent of their lives in school each year in developed countries and:

> Most school effectiveness studies show that 80 per cent or more of student achievement can be explained by student background rather than schools. (Silins and Mulford, 2002: page 561)

In many respects schools are marginal to overall educational outcomes. They can be very good indeed at academic outcomes but obviously these are only a small part of what it means to be an educated person. Broader issues such as life chances and well-being, however measured and defined, are the product of an immensely complex interplay between a wide range of interconnected variables.

For example the role of the family in educational success, by a whole range of criteria, is increasingly well understood and in many respects is greater than that of the school. This leads to the superficially logical notion that instead of improving schools we should be 'improving' families. Equally, the quality of community life (the village) has a direct correlation with well-being and life chances. Social capital is a powerful factor in personal success and is a significant factor in explaining the relative success of schools, as is the level of relative wealth or poverty. Add social class to this equation and it becomes possible to see that in many significant respects the school is a product of its environment and serves to reinforce the prevailing social factors rather than enabling learning irrespective of context. In other words the school might actually exacerbate the factors disadvantaging the individual learner.

Learning can take place anytime, anywhere with anyone

Schools are one of the few social institutions that still operate on what is usually caricatured as the factory system. Under the nineteenth-century factory system – as a broad stereotype – every worker worked on the same way at the same time within a working culture that denied individual choice, responsibility or initiative. Workers started work at the same time, had breaks at the same time and ended at the same time. Overseers and managers did not work to the same patterns and were primarily concerned with applying draconian rules that denied individuality or the dignity of the person. Nowadays, of course, schools have only the vaguest echoes of this culture but the fact remains that schools, in many respects, if they are no longer factories do represent the bureaucratization of learning.

In many ways schooling might be thought of as an essentially rectangular process:

- The architectural plan of a school is essentially a series of rectangles
- The arrangement of desks in classrooms is a permutation of rectangles
- Lessons are often planned as linear blocks
- Schooling is based on a linear curriculum arranged in subject blocks
- Advancement through the school system is by automatic chronological cohort progression

In order to challenge the assumption of homogeneity that underpins many aspects of the schooling experience a range of alternative approaches needs to be considered that will serve to diminish the need for the control element of schooling and enable learners to take on responsibility for their own learning:

- A focus on the need to design learning programmes around the individual as a unique learner rather than as a member of a class or year group. This implies much more than the diagnosis of learning styles: rather, it implies a detailed profile of all the variables that are likely to have an impact on the individual's ability to learn. In medical terms, moving from an x-ray to a full body scan.
- The introduction of programmes to enhance cognitive ability; what might be called the 'cognitive curriculum' that might take the form of a range of interventions to enhance the skills that Gardner outlines above. The content-based curriculum would become the vehicle for the cognitive curriculum rather than, as at present, an end in itself.
- As part of the cognitive curriculum, far greater emphasis needs to be placed on the cultivation of personal and social skills, the concept of emotional intelligence. This has implications for effective learning, the development of social skills, employability and, crucially, the social expression of moral principles.
- A review of our understanding of assessment, both what is assessed and how it is assessed, moving essentially from summative to formative, from assessment of learning to assessment for learning.

- A radical rethinking of the role of the teacher, moving from the manager of information to the facilitator of the learning of the individual. Central to this change is the development of the role of the educator as mentor as the pivotal relationship in the facilitation of learning.
- A focus on the development of ICT to support the learning process, especially the development of cognitive skills such as memorization, problem-solving, analysis and information management. In particular the use of ICT as the basis of managing information, assessment and recording progression.

Conclusion: learning for the future

Based on what has been discussed in this chapter, it is possible to begin to draw some tentative conclusions about what actions might be taken now in order to create a model of learning for the future. The fundamental issue is to create an effective dialogue between professional educators and those carrying out research into all branches of neuroscience and cognitive development. At present, educationalists are working by inference and innuendo, feeding off the crumbs when they need to be sitting at the table as equal participants. There is an obvious need for a radical change in perception as to what constitutes professional knowledge and the creation of new communities of practice centred on the application of scientific research to professional practice in schools. Fundamental to all of these points is an emphasis on the early years of learning; neurologically, socially and morally investment in the early years seems to be the one thing that is most likely to create a learning society.

What is very clear is that schools need to be fundamentally reconceptualized so that they are designed to enable learning – rather than teaching, control or social engineering. Any summary of this debate is bound to be a parody but it is possible to identify a range of implications for educators about research into the brain:

- There is need for a much greater understanding of the development of the brain and cognitive potential in the early years.
- Effective learning is an individual phenomenon – every brain is unique – and there needs to be much more explicit recognition of individual disposition to learn. For example, exploring the implications of the dictum 'stage not age'.
- Teaching needs to pay more attention to the variables influencing engagement with learning, for example, choice of learning activities, time-on-task, appropriate levels of challenge, development of cognitive skills and strategies, especially memory.
- The psychological aspects of learning need greater recognition – even though the effects may be long term. Health is a vital component of effective brain functioning.
- Human relationships, especially in the family, have a profound impact on learning capacity. The emotional state of the learner determines significantly effective neurological functioning.

It would be wrong to underestimate the barriers to the changes outlined in this discussion: the more profound the changes, the more fundamental is the need for leadership that is focused on transformation. However, it is not enough for leaders to increase their knowledge of the areas outlined in this discussion; increasing technical knowledge has to be balanced by an increasing understanding of the ethical issues implicit to any form of research and a robust assertion of the core purposes of education balancing the scientific and technocratic with the humanistic. As currently formulated schools are probably not 'fit for purpose' in terms of learning, nor are they vehicles to achieve social justice – so why do we sustain and perpetuate them?

8 Achieving system-wide school transformation: the argument in brief

David Hopkins

As school systems improve they tend to follow a natural progression. In simple terms, systems that are currently in an 'awful' state need direct and quite prescriptive intervention in order to make progress. In contrast, at the other end of the spectrum, the move from to 'good' to 'great' requires the unleashing of innovativeness and high degrees of school autonomy. In the mid range, the movement from, say, 'adequate' to 'good' implies a gradual rebalancing of top down and bottom up responsibility as seen in Figure 8.1 below. This rebalancing needs to be strategically achieved because the transition from 'prescription' to 'professionalism' necessitates the systematic building of capacity particularly at the school level. This is not to say that there is no longer a role for government, either local or national, during the process of rebalancing, but it will change from being direct and interventionist to challenging and facilitative. It should also still respect the principle of 'reciprocity' whereby the demand for improvement is matched by the supply of support necessary to achieve that improvement.

Figure 8.1 Towards system-wide sustainable reform

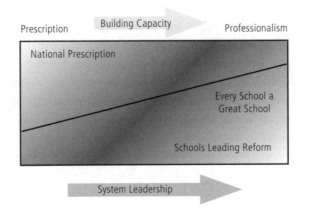

The building of capacity is essential as it is should not be divorced from the continuous improvement of standards of learning and achievement on the part of students. Improvement strategies need to combine both. The attention currently being given to the personalization of learning, the professionalization of teaching, to more formative approaches to accountability and to networking are illustrative of reform initiatives that have the ability to achieve both of these objectives at the same time. Also these four core activities need to be both strategically linked and responsive to context as seen in Figure 8.2 below.

Figure 8.2 Four drivers for building capacity

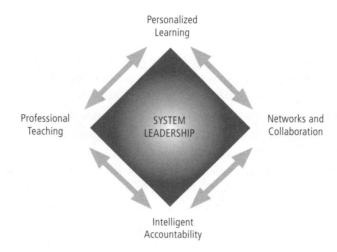

The moulding of what has been called these four 'key drivers' to context is essentially the achievement of leadership at the school level. Although the initiative is often taken by the head of the school, it is the function of leadership and how it is distributed that is important here, not simply the role itself. As an educational system re-balances itself towards 'professionalism' in the move from 'adequate' to 'good' performance, a new style of leadership is seen to emerge. This is now commonly referred to as 'system leadership'. In these instances the school leadership is not just concerned with the internal system of the school and its improvement, although they always are, but they are also mindful of their contribution to the wider system as a whole. A number of distinct yet overlapping 'system leadership roles' are now emerging. For example, there are those headteachers who develop and *lead a successful educational improvement partnership* between several schools or who act as *community leaders*; those who *partner another school facing difficulties* and improve it; those who are *pedagogic and curriculum innovators* who share widely their outstanding practice; and those who work as *change agents* for governmental, national or local organizations.

The English school system has over the past 12 years been involved in a process similar to the one described above. Although the transition has not been as linear or as strategic as has just been outlined, this narrative would be recognizable to most educators. The outcomes have also been impressive: witness the almost 20 per cent gain in literacy and numeracy at the primary level and the year on year gains in GCSE results in secondary schools. But more needs to be done and rapidly. Poverty is still the most significant contributor to poor school performance, as seen in Figure 8.3 below. There is also an unacceptable level of variation within schools (see Figure 8.4) and between schools (see Figure 8.5).

Figure 8.3 Poverty as a contributor to poor school performance

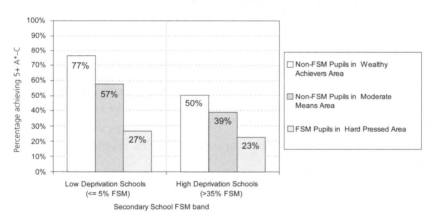

Figure 8.4 Within school variation – Variation in GCSE/GNVQ (ref. bulletin)

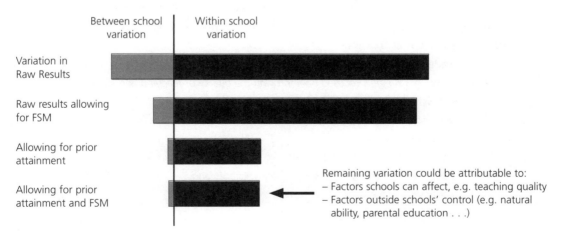

Achieving system-wide school transformation: the argument in brief 63

Figure 8.5 Between school variation

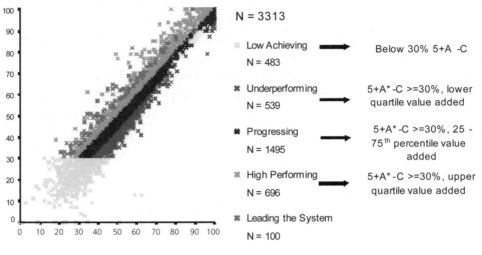

N = 3313

Low Achieving	→	Below 30% 5+A -C
N = 483		
Underperforming	→	5+A* -C >=30%, lower quartile value added
N = 539		
Progressing	→	5+A* -C >=30%, 25 - 75th percentile value added
N = 1495		
High Performing	→	5+A* -C >=30%, upper quartile value added
N = 696		
Leading the System		
N = 100		

Estimated 5+A* -C % from pupil KS3 data

This argues for an intensification of the direction of travel outlined so far, not a return to more direct intervention although this may be necessary in those few individual circumstances where performance is still 'awful' and has to be raised to 'adequate'. But even here, as is argued below, this will be intervention of a type different from what was previously known. Given the systemic orientation of this chapter, the 'intensification' needs to be at two levels:

- The internal system of the school
- Through strategic segmentation enable the system to draw on its own diversity to improve itself

Both have to act in concert for transformation to genuinely occur.

Although the impact of leadership on student achievement and school effectiveness has been acknowledged for some time, it is only recently that we have begun to understand more fully the fine-grained nature of that relationship. A reasonably elegant summary of this evidence is as follows:

- The leadership develops *a narrative for improvement*
- The leadership is *highly focused on improving the quality of teaching and learning* (and student welfare)
- The leadership explicitly *organizes the school for improvement*
- The leadership creates:
    - *clarity (of the systems established)*
    - *consistency (of the systems spread across school), and*
    - *continuity (of the systems over time)*
    - *internal accountability and reciprocity*

- The leadership works to *change context as a key component of their improvement strategy*

There are two relatively new features to this profile. The first is the emphasis on narrative and its impact on both on strategy and culture. It is the nature of narrative that makes it integrative and cumulative, presenting a series of complex and interacting initiatives within a unifying story around the image of a journey. This is strategic in so far as it integrates a wide variety of initiatives and projects forward, and cultural in so far as it speaks both to the individual and collective contribution. The second is the emphasis on 'systems' and the transferability and sustainability of best practice. The characteristics of the 'effective school' have been known for some time, but at a rather high level of generalization. Again we have recently acquired more textured understanding of what these effective practices look like and how they combine together: in a 'whole school design'. We are now at a point when all of the key practices can be presented in an implementable and action oriented-form. Again the key point is twofold: although this knowledge is replicable from setting to setting, it must be integrated in order to have transformational impact. An attempt to convey this idea is presented in Figure 8.6 below.

One final point. Although this best practice knowledge is highly specific and replicable, these principles also need to be enacted according to context, resulting in a unique and distinctive school ethos.

Figure 8.6 Core elements of the design of an effective school

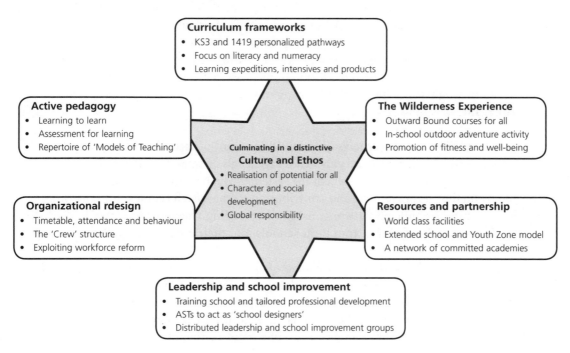

If we want to transform systems as well as schools, then the knowledge encapsulated in the previous paragraph is necessary but not sufficient. It is necessary, indeed essential, because these practices are the critical currency of school improvement. This is the language of school reform. This is inevitably the only focus of the conversations of system leaders, but it has to be coupled to a strategy for system-wide change. It is here where we are on the boundaries of existing knowledge and practice and where national organizations such as the National College for School Leadership can have most impact. It is important to realize however that this aspiration of system transformation being facilitated by the degree of segmentation existing in the system only holds when certain conditions are in place. There are two crucial aspects to this:

- First, that there is increased clarity on the nature of intervention and support for schools at each phase of the performance cycle.
- Second, that schools at each phase are clear as to the most productive ways in which to collaborate in order to capitalize on the diversity within the system.

To understand the dynamics involved we need to return to Figure 8.5. Every secondary school in England, total 3,313, is represented on the diagram in a category related to its effectiveness in terms of student achievement at age 16. The six categories are as follows:

Leading schools (possibly 10 per cent of secondary schools) – these are the highest performing schools that also have the capacity to lead others. Their route to further improvement and contribution to the system comes in at least two forms: first, becoming leading practitioners through disseminating best practice and networking; and second, through working more formally and systematically with lower performing schools through some 'federation' arrangement to improve the partner school's performance.

Succeeding, self-improving schools (possibly 20 per cent of secondary schools) – these are schools that have consistently above average levels of value-added and that exhibit aspects of best practice that will benefit the system through further dissemination. Their route to further improvement and contribution to the system comes in networking their best practice in local networks using their leading teachers to mentor in other schools and to take students from local schools into their areas of specialism.

Succeeding schools but with significant areas of underperformance (possibly 20 per cent of secondary schools) – these schools, although successful on published criteria, have unacceptable numbers of underperforming teachers or departments who are masked by the averaging out of published results. Their route to further improvement and contribution to the system comes on the one hand contributing as above to other schools from their areas of strength and being the recipients of such support in their weaker areas.

Underperforming schools (possibly 25 per cent of secondary schools) – defined as those secondary schools in their lowest value-added quartile of their distribution, who may have adequate or good headline results, but are consistently failing to add value to the progress of their students. Their route to further improvement is to use the data discussed with the School Improvement Partner (SIP) as a basis of a whole school raising standards plan. They will need sustained consultancy in the early stages of an improvement process from a school(s) with a similar intake, but far higher value added using a modified version of a 'federation intervention'.

Low attaining schools (possibly 20 per cent of secondary schools) – defined as those secondary schools below the 30 per cent A*–C GCSE floor target but with a capacity to improve. Their route to further improvement requires sustained support through some federation arrangement or involvement, consultancy support through the National Challenge and possibly the application of an improvement grant.

Failing schools (possibly 5 per cent of secondary schools) – defined as being well below the floor target and with little capacity to improve. At a minimum these schools will require intervention in the form of a 'hard federation' or membership of the Intensive Support Programme. If these strategies are not successful in the short term, then closure, Academy status or a school's competition is the only other answer in order to sustain adequate provision for the students involved.

A summary of this approach is set out in the following table. In the right-hand column is a basic taxonomy of schools based on the previous analysis. The number of categories and the terminology will vary from setting to setting, the crucial point being that not all schools are the same and each requires different forms of support. It is this that is the focus of the second column, where a range of strategies for supporting schools at different phases of their development is briefly described. Again these descriptions are grounded in the English context, but they do have a more universal applicability. There are three key points here:

- The first is that one size does not fit all.
- The second that these different forms of intervention and support are increasingly being provided by schools themselves, rather than being imposed and delivered by some external agency. This approach to system transformation relies fundamentally on school-to-school support as the basis of the improvement strategy.
- The third is that this process can continue to evolve in an *ad hoc* way or it can be orchestrated by a national organization with strong local roots such as the NCSL or the SSAT. The blank third column conveys this potential.

Type of school	Key strategies – responsive to context and need	Policy lever
Leading schools	Become leading practitioners Formal federation with lower performing schools	?
Succeeding, self-improving schools	Regular local networking for school leaders Between-school curriculum development	?
Succeeding schools with internal variations	Consistency interventions: such as Assessment for Learning Subject specialist support to particular departments	?
Underperforming schools	Linked school support for underperforming departments Underperforming pupil programmes: catch-up	?
Low attaining schools	Formal support in federation structure Consultancy in core subjects and best practice	?
Failing schools	Intensive Support Programme New provider such as an Academy	?

However, in order to be successful this 'segmentation approach' to system transformation requires a fair degree of boldness in setting system level expectations and conditions. There are four implications in particular that have to be grappled with:

- All failing and underperforming (and potentially low achieving) schools should have a leading school that works with them in either a formal grouping federation (where the leading school principal or head assumes overall control and accountability) or in more informal partnership. Evidence from existing federations, where the approach to replication described earlier was adopted, suggests that a national system of federations would be capable of delivering a sustainable step-change in improvement in relatively short periods of time. For example, a number of 'federated schools' have improved their 5 A*–Cs at GCSE from under 20 per cent to over 50 per cent in two years.
- Schools should take greater responsibility for neighbouring schools so that the move towards networking encourages groups of schools to form collaborative arrangements outside of local control. This would be on the condition that these schools provided extended services for all students within a geographic area, but equally on the acceptance that there would be incentives for doing so. Encouraging local schools to work together will build capacity for continuous improvement at local level.
- The incentives for greater system responsibility should include significantly enhanced funding for students most at risk to counter the predictive character of poverty noted earlier. Beyond incentivizing local collaboratives, the potential effects for large-scale long-term reform include:
  - A more even distribution of 'at risk' students and associated increases in standards, due to more schools seeking to admit a larger proportion of 'at risk' students so as to increase their overall income.

- A significant reduction in 'sink schools' even where 'at risk' students are concentrated, as there would be much greater potential to respond to the social-economic challenges (for example, by paying more to attract the best teachers; or by developing excellent parental involvement and outreach services).

- A rationalization of national and local agency functions and roles to allow the higher degree of national and regional co-ordination for this increasingly devolved system. At present there are too many national and local organizations acting in a competitive, unco-ordinated and capricious way.

Note:

An earlier version was prepared for the Specialist Schools and Academies Trust and the argument is developed in detail in Hopkins, D. (2007), *Every School a Great School*, Maidenhead: McGraw-Hill/ Open University Press.

9 Future leadership: challenges and implications

Alma Harris

Introduction

In the struggle to transform educational systems in many countries, one thing is clear –we need new ways of thinking about educational change and new organizational forms that make educational systems self-renewing. Our past attempts at large-scale reform have tended to constrain system level change by focusing on competition as the main lever for raising performance. It is now clear that the returns from this approach are diminishing and new approaches are needed to transform schooling in the twenty-first century.

The new educational order is rapidly changing. The ability to work and lead beyond the individual school is of increasing importance. Partnerships between schools and other professional groups and sectors will continue to dominate the landscape for the foreseeable future. Therefore 'new models of leadership' are required to meet these demands. The main drivers for developing alternative models of leadership are:

- Succession and pipeline issues plus workload
- Diversity of schools and partnership arrangements
- Link between leadership and learning i.e. improved student outcomes
- ECM, Extended Schools and Children's Plan

The key argument in this chapter is that twenty-first century schooling necessitates a shift away from vertical, policy-driven change to *lateral, capacity building* change. Strategic collaboration and a focus on building social capital and relational trust within, between and across schools and partner organizations is the key to system re-design and system transformation.

Schools are becoming more complex places. In the future they will need to be more responsive to a rapidly changing environment and set of circumstances. They will need to be *highly adaptable* structures that are versatile and responsive to shifting needs and priorities. Therefore the leadership practice has to also be adaptive, flexible and highly responsive to external and internal imperatives for change.

The current leadership structures in our schools are no longer fit the needs of twenty-first century schooling. There is growing evidence of schools changing structures, roles and responsibilities but they are still constrained by the formalized leadership structure that imposes a certain way of working. It reinforces leadership as role and position, rather than leadership as practice. Current leadership and future leadership can be characterized as follows:

Current leadership	Future leadership
Hierarchical and fixed	Lateral and interchangeable
Role and position	Talent and capability
Located in one school	Movement around schools
Problem based	Solution focused
Skills	Practice
Control and efficiency	Capacity building and relational capital
Focused on organization	Focused on instruction
Linked to remuneration	Linked to professional growth

The intention here is not to polarize one type of leadership as good or bad but to try to look at ways in which leadership can become aligned more closely to the needs of twenty-first century schooling. In the book *The Wisdom of Crowds* James Surowiecki argues that 'diversity helps because it actually adds perspectives that would otherwise be absent'. This suggests that the potential for imaginative and creative solutions to problems is more likely to occur where there is diversity of leadership practice that fits the contours or the needs of the organization or system. Ron Heifetz (1994) focused attention on the idea of an adaptive challenge where solutions lie outside the current way of operating. It is suggested that the leadership we now require is outside our current way of operating.

New models of schooling = new leadership practices

The education system in England is currently being redefined in terms of new forms of partnership and new types of schools. It is predicated on greater freedom and autonomy for schools and the system as a whole. This new model of schooling will inevitably require new forms of leadership and decision-making processes that are *widely distributed* within, between and across schools plus partner organizations. It will require leadership that is distributed across into the community in its widest and most diverse sense. It will require:

- Leadership that crosses structural, cultural and personal barriers
- Leadership that builds capacity within schools, communities and systems
- Leadership that generates relational and social capital
- Leadership that sustains performance
- Leadership that supports re-design and self-renewal

But there is a fault line. Despite knowing that we need new models of leadership we are still perpetuating the existing models. We continue to provide conventional leadership solutions to complex leadership problems. There is a shortage of heads – but why rush to fill the vacancies, why not think of this as an opportunity for a different approach to leading our schools? Are the current leadership roles still fit for purpose? With different professionals now working with and within our schools, does the role of 'headteacher' still make sense? If we are serious about school transformation this can only be secured through abandoning previous practice and actively re-designing schooling.

In his book *Cognition in the Wild* Edward Hutchings talks about the forms of effective communication and learning with a large and complex organization – a naval ship. His basic premise is that the ship functions as a learning community, collectively solving problems through shared expertise and knowledge. The interdependence of the individual and the environment means that human activity is *distributed in the interactive web of actors, artefacts and the situation* (Spillane, 2006). This distributed cognition is what Hutchings equates with *effective system learning*.

While the world of a twenty-first century school may be very different from that of a naval ship they are both highly complex social systems that require distributed leadership to function most effectively.

New leadership practices = distributed leadership

Distributed leadership underlines the importance of collective knowledge and understanding and emphasizes that leadership is most effective in complex systems when it is *distributed and shared*. Leadership distribution is a sophisticated vehicle for knowledge transfer and knowledge creation. But what exactly is meant by distributed leadership?

In one sense all leadership is distributed. As the power of influence and direction is felt at different levels within any organization this could be seen as distributed leadership. However, to understand distributed leadership beyond this simplistic notion means highlighting a number of important points. Distributed leadership implies that leadership practice is *broad based*, *stretched* and *extended* within, across and between schools (Harris, 2008). Distributed leadership is primarily concerned with mobilizing leadership at all levels not just relying on leadership from the top. The emphasis is upon leadership as *interaction and practice* rather than relying upon the actions associated those in formal leadership role or responsibilities.

A distributed model of leadership is one premised upon capacity building and talent management. It has a number of key features:

- Distributed leadership is primarily concerned with capacity building
- Distributed leadership can only be promoted, it cannot be mandated
- Distributed leadership is inclusive and implies broad-based involvement in leadership practice

- Distributed leadership does not mean everybody leads but rather that everybody has the potential to lead, at some time
- Distributed leadership occurs in various patterns, there is no blueprint
- Distributed leadership requires deep trust and reciprocal support
- Distributed leadership is a form of leadership premised upon utilizing the talent and capabilities of those within the school and outside it
- Distributed leadership is concerned with two things:
  - *The process of leadership* – how leadership occurs within the organization
  - *Leadership activity* – how leadership is enhanced and developed

In very practical terms distributed leadership is deliberately orchestrated. Heads and other leaders actively orchestrate the internal organizational conditions for distributed leadership to thrive. By providing the time, space and opportunity for different staff to meet, plan and reflect, alternative sources of leadership are generated. By offering staff opportunities to lead, and by providing the creative spaces for dialogue and discussion within across and between schools, leadership capacity is created.

Implications

Brian Caldwell (2006) talks about the 'new image of the self-managing school' as being one where the student is the most important unit of the organization – not the classroom or the school. He argues that schools cannot achieve transformation by acting alone or operating in a line of support from the centre of the school system, to the school, to the department to the classroom. The success of the school, he suggests depends *upon its capacity to join networks or federations to share knowledge, address problems and pool resources.* (Caldwell, 2006:75).

As Hopkins et al (2009) highlight, meeting the contemporary challenges of schooling will require school leaders to 'consider new models of leadership and governance to appropriately distribute an increasing range of responsibilities to a wider and differentiated pool of leadership expertise' (page 9). But there are a number of important considerations:

Distance: As schools grow and become more complex organizations through various partnerships and collaborations with other schools, the issue of distance makes it more difficult for teams to meet and problem solve. The physical space and distance can be a barrier to distributing leadership as the geographic separation makes it more difficult for teachers to connect. The challenge for schools and networks is to provide new, alternative ICT-based solutions to the barrier of distance and to break the boundaries through alternative forms of communication.

Culture: Distributing leadership essentially means a shift in culture away from the 'top down' model of leadership to a form of leadership that is more organic, spontaneous and more difficult to control. It means a departure from a view of leadership that resides in one person to a more sophisticated and complex notion of leadership as a distributed property. The challenge for those in schools and networks is to see leadership as an organizational resource that is maximized through interactions between individuals and teams that leads to problem solving and new developments.

Structure: The way schools are currently organized presents a major set of barriers to distributing leadership. The structure of schooling is still dominated by compartmentalizing subjects, pupils and learning into discrete but manageable boxes. Distributing leadership implies the erosion of these artificial barriers and implies a more fluid way of schools operating. The challenge for schools and networks is to find ways of removing those organizational structures and systems that restrict organizational learning.

Leaders of the future will be part of multiple, multi-disciplinary teams that cross organizational boundaries and professional fault lines. Therefore, there are a number of implications for leadership development. Leadership development of the future is likely to concentrate much more on skills such as *building relationships, cultivating trust, growing talent, organizational re-design and harnessing innovation*. If there is leadership coaching and mentoring it will be at the point of need and it will need to be highly context specific.

The flexibility across different boundaries and the interchange of roles will mean a blurring of the informal/formal leadership interface that currently exists. Instead greater interchange and overlap between *lateral and vertical* forms of leadership practice will require leaders with multiple skills so that they can take on different roles and responsibilities within and across different structures.

Future school leadership will ultimately be 'one learner ahead'. It will be primarily and chiefly concerned with knowledge creation and producing innovation that allows learning for all students to be maximized. This will mean continual re-design and reinvention to ensure that student learning is always at an optimum level.

Future leaders will need to continually monitor the changing external environment. They will need to 'look out of the window' and watch for changing trends or indications that the organization must rethink its strategy or re-position itself. It will have to ensure that the internal leadership patterns, relationship and connections are best arranged to respond decisively and quickly.

Final comment

It is abundantly clear that the idea of what constitutes a 'school' is dramatically and irrecoverably changing. The 24/7 virtual learning environment is no longer a distant aspiration or dream. Young people are now learning through a variety of media, at any time of the day or night, and can receive immediate feedback on progress, from tutors or teachers, anywhere in the world. Within this hi-tech maelstrom, schools are actively re-designing themselves. They recognize that to meet the educational needs of future generations, who take rapid technological change for granted, will require a radical change in the configuration of schooling. Leaders within schools are rapidly realizing that the future models of leadership will be very different from those that characterized the schools of the past.

Increasingly, school leaders will be working in a climate of uncertainty and unpredictable change as the system readjusts and realigns itself to the demands of twenty-first century teaching and learning. This will undoubtedly mean the abandonment of previous ways of working and the adoption of new practices in a much shorter timeframe of innovation than ever before. The unit of change is no longer the school or the system but the individual learner with his or her own personalized learning pathway. In the fluid, boundary-less school of the future, what will leadership look like, how will it function, how will it be understood? What are the implications for leadership development and for leadership practice that crosses professional boundaries? What forms of training and development will educational leaders require to be effective?

To answer these questions requires returning to distributed leadership. Schools of the future are more likely to require multiple rather than individual leaders. As organizations become more complex, diffuse and networked, various forms of direction and influence will be required to respond to quickly shifting and changing environments. Multiple sources or points of leadership will be needed within the organization to ensure it is both sensitive and responsive to change. The leadership patterns of the future will be determined by the configuration of the network of provision. The complex nature of organizations will mean that the co-ordination of leadership activity will most likely be undertaken both laterally and vertically and leadership functions and responsibilities will fluctuate with the changing needs of the organization.

Future leadership will no longer be divided into fixed roles and responsibilities. Patterns of leadership responsibility will ebb and flow. Leadership functions and actions will depend on organizational need and patterns of leadership activity will need to be flexible enough to regroup and remobilize around particular issues or areas for development. Leadership of the future will be driven much more by internal accountability than by external accountability frameworks. With broader and more distributed forms of leadership activity there will be more opportunity to pick up early signals within the organization of any potential destabilization. With more emphasis upon internal accountability, leaders at all levels will be much more focused on developing the practice of teaching and learning than the routine management of these processes.

Educational organizations of the future will be networked, diffuse and partly virtual. For each learner there will be a different configuration of learning support, an individualized and personalized learning programme. Therefore leadership of the future will be primarily concerned with maximizing synergies and connectivity across different parts of the learning network or system. It will not be focused on the results of individual parts of the organization but will be more interested in the performance of the whole. Attention will be paid to maximizing leadership capability and capacity-building within and between organizational forms.

We undoubtedly, need new forms of leadership as we step into the dynamic but uncharted territory of twenty-first century learning. We need new ways of understanding, analyzing and making sense of change. We need alternative perspectives on leadership activity. Distributed leadership offers one such perspective. It certainly isn't a panacea or blueprint for system transformation but there are indications from contemporary research of a positive relationship between distributed forms of leadership and organizational/student outcomes. Recent evidence has underscored that distributed leadership contributes to the development of academic capacity and also contributes indirectly to student learning outcomes (Hallinger, 2009). These findings, and many others, provide growing empirical support for a call for the development of a broader capacity to lead within schools.

As schooling becomes more differentiated, networked and extended it is difficult to see how current leadership structures can be retained. Many schools are already re-designing themselves and are actively changing their leadership practices. They are engaged in sophisticated forms of distributed leadership activity that extend beyond professional boundaries and traditional demarcation. The central challenge now is to develop, foster and actively encourage new, diverse and distributed models of leadership that take the entire system forward and upwards. This won't be achieved by holding on to leadership structures suited, and indeed intended, for another age.

10 Community renaissance

Paul Clarke

This chapter explores the development of community, within which our idea of 'school' is currently located. When we think about the future relationship between the community and school, it seems to me that community is what will be developed, and what develops it will be learning. The chapter will suggest that it is only through thinking about community as a forum for development of interdependencies that we have any real possibility of making progress with the urgent agenda for a more sustainable form of life on the planet. If we are to enhance our capability to learn new ways of living which have a reduced footprint on the environment of the planet, I think we have to consider how we redefine our relationship with a dominant community-based institution – *the school*. This takes us beyond our current idea of building schools for the future, into an exploration of renaissance of community for the future.

I suggest that the development of community is not to be defined as new buildings and priorities imposed through government reforms, nor as recycled ideas of the old model of school, but as a set of interdependencies which may be practised face to face, or through the new opportunities open to us through technology. These interdependencies come in the form of individual engagement, through connection with ideas and shared interests, and through collective action in the pursuit of new freedoms. As Sen (1999) argues, 'Greater freedom enhances the ability of people to help themselves and also to influence the world, and these matters are central to the process of development' (page 18). As such, I am interested in a new economic model, or more particularly an eco-economy (Brown, 2002) or what is also called eco-eco (Kelly, 2009) where development of community is the practice of sustainable development.

In the chapter I will use 'community' as the term which captures a set of capabilities (Sen, 1999). One where we depend upon each other to generate understanding, engagement and participation and through which we can respond to social, environmental and economic collapse (Putnam, 2000; Orr, 1994; Soros, 2008). I describe the concept of community as a network. It is an interdependent construct of human activity. Community functions as the manifestation of a set of capabilities within and between communities of connection, communities of place, communities of interest and communities of action. Learning plays a significant part in framing our definitions of community and the capabilities that sustain communities, sometimes impeding, sometimes enabling and focusing the development of these capabilities. Historically the school is located at the interconnect of these capabilities. However, increasingly the school is a part player; the setting is always within the wider social context of the community and as such, learning takes its place (see Figure 10.1).

Community is both boundaried and at the same time is boundless. We live our lives largely dependent on systems which have no respect for national boundaries, such as the atmosphere, oceans, ocean life, biotic provinces and the sun, without which nothing lives. All these natural structures demonstrate forms of community interdependence which function as flow, an entangled alliance. This illustrates sufficiently that community can exist as something visible and tangible and at the same time something abstract.

This forms the basis of much of my own work, exploring the practicalities of new forms of what I have come to call 'local dependency' (Clarke, 2009) where example can be drawn from what happens in one location and can serve as a stimulus to develop new ideas and new activity in another. Since our world is increasingly connected through cultural, economic and technological mechanisms, and proportionally ever less physical, the meaning of 'local' is not geographical, at least not *only* geographical. It explores the ways in which flows of ideas combine as communities in the form of practices, theories and possibilities to be realized as forms of wealth as environmental capital (Clarke, 2009), human capital, social capital, spiritual capital, manufactured capital and financial capital (Porritt, 2009) – the flow is between people sharing and playing with these things both in real-time together, separately and, at times, virtually in their own time

Figure 10.1 Capabilities of an interdependent community

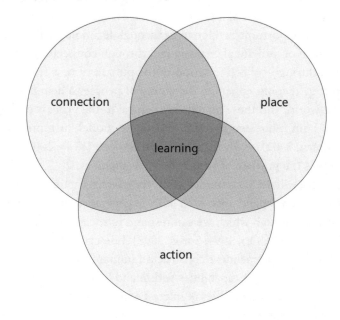

Sen (1999) describes the qualities of collective action which widen the opportunity for individuals to generate forms of wealth as 'capabilities'. It is a combination of these capabilities in the form of dependencies of what I call *connection, place* and *action* that I wish to explore when we move forward in our consideration of the role and function of a relationship between community and new forms of learning.

A community of connection

Governments, regions, communities and individuals are beginning to recognize the scale of the environmental challenge that human beings face in this century as we have to make the move from an oil-based industrialized economy to an ecologically focused post-oil economy (Steffen, 2008). This transition is starting to happen and recent predictions suggest that it will have to have completed within 50 years regardless of whether we want it or not, as oil is rapidly running out and a looming prospect of energy shortage and blackouts gets ever closer[1].

While the twentieth century is now well behind us, we have not as yet learned how to live, yet alone think in terms of actions and relationships, in the mindset we might need for life in the twenty-first. This should not be all that difficult, as the dominant ideas of the economic and political model from the twentieth century have clearly just fallen apart around us in the last two decades and the lessons are there for all to see. These models have until now been looked upon as mutually exclusive, the failure of Soviet state socialism in the 1990s, and now Western market-driven capitalism have both defined in their own ways, the failed ideologies of national systems. However, as Hobsbawm (2009) argues, both are 'bankrupt ideas' when we contemplate our futures. We need a progressive model to transcend the old order and respond to the new situation in which we find ourselves.

One particular feature of both of these 'bankrupt' models, is the reliance upon institutions to perpetuate particular ideological viewpoints. Ivan Illich (1975) argued that modern societies across the industrialized world appear to create more and more institutions, and that the consequence of them is that we live our lives in ever more institutionalized ways. This makes it difficult for people to challenge the existing order of things or to suggest, and to have taken seriously, the idea that there are alternative ways of living.

> This process undermines people – it diminishes their confidence in themselves, and in their capacity to solve problems... It kills convivial relationships. Finally it colonizes life like a parasite ...that kills creativity (Finger and Asú 2001: page 10).

Institutions do other things too. They create experts. The book *Medical Nemesis* (1975) began, 'The medical establishment has become a major threat to health' (Ilich, 1975: page 11). In much of my work I maintain a similar argument, that the *educational establishment has become a major threat to education* (Clarke, 2008). The case against expert systems is that they produce a form of damage which outweighs the potential benefits they offer, because they obscure and collude with the political conditions that render society schooled but ill-educated, and they perpetuate the idea that people are unable to act for themselves. They diminish the power of individuals to learn and value their personal and social experience of learning themselves, the means by which they might shape and improve their own community.

This problem of expert systems becomes particularly acute when there is a need to redefine the relationships that exist between school and community. Here, the institutional boundaries and structures can compromise the institutional potential to learn from the community, its default position being that the school educates the community and not the other way around. Despite plenty of examples that refute this claim, particularly coming from recent changes in communications technology (Leadbeater 2000), the underlying cultural message from schools remains the same, 'We know, you don't know, how to educate.'

It seems to me that, as a result, community and school are stuck in a perpetual cycle of dependency of the worst possible kind. One where professionals and the schools in which they work tend to define the activity of learning as a commodity which they call education, 'whose production they monopolize, whose distribution they restrict, and whose price they raise beyond the purse of ordinary people and nowadays, all governments' (Lister in Illich, 1976), and the community receives the product. Extending an earlier notion of schooling, it might be suggested therefore that people are conditioned to believe that the self-taught *community* is being discriminated against; that learning and the growth of cognitive capacity require a process of consumption of services presented in a planned, professional form (quoted by Gajardo, 1994: page 715; my insert of *community*) In this way, learning is a *commodity* rather than an *activity*, so any way in which a community might attempt to engage with a school is inhibited by its inability to present a form of knowledge to the school in a recognizable, and therefore acceptable, professional manner.

Just like cigarettes, institutions and institutional practices would appear to be addictive. The fact that school is perceived to be compulsory may be significant here – as institutions, schools generate habitual activities and rituals and these are difficult to quit once people get hooked on the idea that they are the only way to behave or to solve existing problems. If, as individuals and *communities*, we can develop the capabilities to distinguish between what we want and what we understand to be a requirement, we can use such capability to make proactive choices, acting as agents rather than consumers of learning.

Having grown conditioned to schooling of a certain type (Orr, 1994), the action of individuals, communities, regions and countries to overcome the challenges we face from economic and ecological meltdown demand the cleverest of inventions, the smartest of technologies, and the most politic and decorous of societies. The current landscape of challenges offers immense potential for people to work together in new ways to form new types of economic well-being which serve both personal and societal needs (Porritt, 2009).

By challenging the process of institutionalization, by questioning the established notions of expertise and experts and by critiquing the idea of learning as a form of commodity, we should be able to move towards a way of living and working in our communities where collective wisdom is captured and focused with clarity and purpose and without the embedded issues of ownership and power getting in the way; where people have a clear sense of the purpose behind the initiatives which serve self and others and indeed the well understood needs of the community as a whole. A transition in thinking about how to live in the twenty-first century that redefines wealth in the form of environmental capital (Clarke 2009), human capital, social capital, spiritual capital, cultural and creative capital, manufactured capital and financial capital needs mediation. The basic ideas need to be explored and discussed, from which practical actions can flow.

A 'community of connection' that develops capabilities to appreciate and engage with alternative solutions, designs and opportunities and which values the very process of connecting meaningfully with others, helps us to think differently and enables us to respond to the eco-eco (Kelly, 2009) demands of the twenty-first century. This model of community serves as a frame for thinking about the contributing factors which inform a dialogue for transforming the relationship between community and school.

A community of place

In a similar way to the failings of the macro system, the micro-level is not without its problems (Klein, 2001). While state-led reform of 'communities' continues to illustrate systemic failings through the alienation and disengagement of the majority of those this hoped for reform is intended to assist, other, equally problematic, issues arise when the alternatives being pursued are for self-sufficient purposes. As an idea, the notion of self-sufficient communities has done just as much harm than as good. It perpetuates the 'otherness' of those beyond one's own clique, and it generates economic inequality just as efficiently as any macro market-led solution. The self-sufficiency argument extends now into our current school model. While defined primarily through school choice, it is just as much about exclusivity and self-sufficiency. Academies, Trust and Foundation schools are quite possibly the next failed extension of the industrialized, individualized cultural obsession with privacy and isolationist solutions to large-scale problems. They are the macro solution to micro challenge and they perpetuate the myth that a new building with a new name (Academy, Foundation) will redefine the relationship between it, as an institution, and the community in which it exists. 'We don't need you, we are self-sufficient, we generate our own solutions' is as much a lie as that which argues that we can only make cultural, environmental and economic progress with government. The message is clear, there is no dissectable self, we depend on each other. It is therefore a maturation towards some other form of interdependency, one which connects rather than dissects self from community and from wider networks, that we urgently need to develop.

So a community of place is particularly important as a way of making sense of the important role school plays *within* a social context. When one's environment has a 'sustained and lasting human value' (O'Sullivan, 1999) the result of the individualized and commodified version of globalization, rootlessness, transitoriness and dispossession become more and not less transparent (ibid: page 245). The dependence by people on a community of place becomes in itself a value. Place is often cited as a significantly important feature of schools in locations of economic disadvantage, where, in the best examples, students are embedded into activity which helps to develop capability in the forms of environmental capital, human capital, social capital, spiritual capital, creative and cultural capital, manufactured capital and financial capital. However, just as the community of place can be a physical reality it can also demonstrate capability in the form of a virtual reality. Take, for example, the degree of interest young people have in Facebook, Bebo and other social networking sites.

Our capability to create and maintain a sense of place within a community–school relationship therefore explores both physical and virtual realities. To be successful it needs to generate capabilities which include a sense of identity, a need for love, care, protection, affection, understanding, participation, creativity and friendship.

Community as action

A particular form of community capability is often found in and around schools in the form of active groups that pursue specific projects on behalf of the school such as community liaison, parental outreach, after-school and breakfast clubs all of which illustrate the commodity function of school. While they are interesting and in some cases quite powerful examples of ways in which relationships can be developed between school and community, they do not go far enough to illustrate the capability in which I am particularly interested because it seems to me that they maintain, rather than transform, the possibility of greater levels of interdependence.

However, there are some interesting examples of community as action which are showing signs of significantly contributing to the redesign of existing systems. In one example, an action community in the form of a local food production project approached a school to form a community interest company (CIC) which is joint owned between school and community trustees. The CIC applied for, and won, a significant lottery fund which is establishing a sustainable fish farm eco-business on the school site. The students from the school, working with a number of local businesses and regional agencies, are actively involved in all stages of design, commissioning, construction, maintenance and development of the business. There are new school courses being established in land management and eco energy, which will run within the school and the local college.

Alongside people from the immediate vicinity of the town who are helping to support and provide guidance, there are students and lecturers from university departments from other countries who have experience of developing this type of farm with associated aquaponics and filtration systems.

Furthermore, to illustrate the idea of community as connection, place and action, the town has partnerships with other communities in Ghana and Tanzania that are involved in knowledge transfer, planning and development conversations as they are undertaking similar projects in their localities.

Conclusion

This chapter has attempted to provide a stimulus for a different way of thinking about the complicated issue of school and community. Instead of suggesting more of the same, I have argued that we need to radically realign our concept to take full advantage of the types of capabilities we might need to encourage if we are to truly transform our education system to meet the changing demands of an eco-eco society.

I have suggested that the future of sustainable economy and community depends on the connections we choose, the place we define as local, and the life we subsequently decide to live in the form of deliberate action.

The implications of this type of reform are considerable. In conclusion, it is worth thinking about some of the challenges and posing some questions.

Capability building for communities. What would need to happen if these kind of changes were to be brought about in disenfranchised communities which are characterized by an absence of collective vision, aspiration or leadership? Who would take responsibility for the development of the 'capabilities' that would be necessary for the first steps of positive action? This could generate a new role for school – a model of learning as community capability building, where the school has as much responsibility for developing the wider *context* for learning (i.e, the community and the connected members within it) as it does for the process or activity of learning (teaching).

In the chapter I have briefly referred to the radical change in the perceptions of educators of themselves as *experts*. Any profession under fire (as teachers always seem to be) clings onto its 'expert' status as a last resort in the face of change. Unless the practical and attitudinal changes required to bring about this new vision for a sustainable learning ecology are acknowledged we may find ourselves locked into the increasingly desperate version of 'sustainability training' as another bolt-on reform. An exploration of the capabilities that teachers may need to help them to contribute to community capability seems a practical way to proceed.

It seems that a deeper consideration of values may be useful in seeking to bring about such change. While a great deal of the thrust of my argument centres around the impending disaster and possible response anticipated when the oil runs out, we may usefully engage people more fully in the debate through a broader consideration of the need for change. This discussion could include:

- The need for greater social cohesion
- The need for improved physical and mental well-being
- The need for greater personal agency and active citizenship
- The need for greater social justice and equality
- The need to address 'crisis' issues such as crime, poverty, etc.

I would also suggest that it is through deep consideration of the values that drive and shape our education system that change might be more widely justified or rationalized. When people think about re-visioning education they often ask 'What kind of young adults do we want to see as a result of this process?' and those imaginings are shaped by a set of values. At the moment the vision is limited and largely defined by government, as is the tradition in education – primarily by the values associated with economic productiveness. Perhaps the question needs to shift to 'What kind of community do we want our schools to build as they redefine their service to others?'

We urgently need the process of learning to be meaningfully integrated into the social, the community context, and for learning transactions (the process of education) to be more closely aligned with the transactions that are more widely necessary for the development of sustainable communities and societies.

Notes

1 'Shell estimates that after 2015 supplies of easy-to-access oil and gas will no longer keep up with demand' Jeroen van de Veer, CEO of Shell, leaked e-mail to executive board 22 January 2008, sourced for this chapter in *Preparing for Peak Oil: Local Authorities and the Energy Crisis*. (2008), London: Oil Depletion Analysis Centre

2 *Guardian* 16 April 2009 (page 27). Nuclear plans 'too slow to stop lights going out.'

3 For detailed quantitative data on oil depletion rates see also Birol, F. (2008), *World Energy Outlook*. Paris: International Energy Agency.

11 The global context of local school leadership

Raphael Wilkins

Introduction

This chapter explores how education systems can balance local, national and global agendas. It is concerned with globalization and the future of schooling, with a focus on constitutional relations between levels of governance (national, local and institutional), and the political realities that drive national policy. I will argue that the reconciliation of local and global agendas can only be achieved with a contribution of proactive local leadership.

This is not a report of empirical research: I am drawing on reflective analysis of my own experience both as a system leader in UK education and as a policy adviser and lobbyist at national level, combined with scholarship in relevant fields. I write in the first person to acknowledge that my argument is influenced both by my professional journey, working in different contexts of education policy and leadership, and by my intellectual journey, as I have tried to map out these matters sufficiently to see some possible routes forward.

Globalization and education futures

The topics 'globalization' and 'education futures' are separate but related. Some of the elements that make up the phenomenon of globalization, such as intercontinental trade, communication and migration, and the mixing of ideas between different cultures, have a very long history. Use of the term started to become significant around 30 years ago, in response to the developments of the time which have continued apace. So globalization can be studied as a historical or current phenomenon as well as being a field for speculation about the future. Debate about 'education futures' is concerned with what education will be like, or ought to be like, in the future: while globalization is a major factor influencing how people envisage future education, this topic embraces other more local considerations as well.

Burbules and Torres (2000) summarized the main features of globalization as the emergence of supranational institutions; the impact of global economic processes; an increased political belief in market forces and deregulation ('neo-liberalism'); and the emergence of global media and technologies of communication. They noted that 'globalization' can also be:

> A construction used by state policymakers to inspire support for, and suppress opposition to, changes because 'greater forces'…leave the nation state 'no choice' but to play by a set of global rules not of its own making. (Burbules and Torres, 2000: page 2)

Burbules and Torres argued that the globalized culture has embraced only certain segments of (global) society, while other segments have been affected less, or differently, by access to global markets and cosmopolitan cultures. They considered the effects of globalization on education to be complex and variable, not falling into neat generalizations or dichotomies. They also challenged assumptions of inevitability about the nature and effects of some of the changes:

> we want to present a corrective to the enthusiasts of globalisation and suggest that even as these changes occur, they can change in different, more equitable and more just ways. (Burbules and Torres, 2000: page 2)

A similarly critical stance might be applied to projections of what education will be like in the future, both as to the inevitability and uniformity of change. One strand of thinking treats the school system as a 'technology' which has become outdated. This line of thinking has compared the schoolhouse of the nineteenth century with the factories of the same period and argued that, because in certain industries the factories have been replaced by completely new technologies, the school system is outdated and should use information and communications technology (ICT) to undergo a similar level of metamorphosis (for example, Hargreaves 1994).

I question the notion that the correct 'technological' comparison for schools is with nineteenth-century factories or with modern, large-scale industrial processes. Schools and schooling have existed in recognizable form for a much longer period than industrial processes. The basic concept of a lesson in a classroom provided by a teacher to a group of pupils is as old as civilization. The exhibits in the National School Museum in Rotterdam, of teaching and learning from the time of Charlemagne to the present day, show that over recent centuries the schoolroom has undergone a gradual evolution. In its style, furnishing and some other respects, the development of the schoolroom has run more or less alongside the changes in the homes in which the pupils live. Like the schoolroom, the basic concept of a domestic dwelling place has proved enduring. Given the purposes of schooling, which I discuss later, the question 'What will homes and communities be like in the future?' is at least as relevant to considering the future of education as the question 'What technologies will be used in the future to process chemicals and to run banking systems?'

Another reason for questioning the 'technological' view of the future of education is the diverse impact of change on different sectors of the economy. While it is clearly the case that some industries have been transformed out of recognition, it is also the case that in some sectors of the economy the effects of technological change, while having significance, have not altered the fundamental nature of the activity. Market stallholders, hairdressers, orchestral musicians, painters, actors, child-minders, caterers, hoteliers, athletes, judges, nurses, religious pastors and politicians continue to work in ways that, in their essence, have changed little over the centuries. Perhaps the 'technologies' used in schooling are better compared to those used in these more people-focused sectors of the economy than with industrial processes.

This is not to deny that the technologies of schooling have changed very significantly and will continue to develop in ways that may be difficult to predict. In most schools in the UK, ICT has enabled classroom practice to draw upon different and higher quality educational resources, to employ a wider range of teaching and learning methods, to increase external connections including with other schools nationally and internationally, and to mechanize functions such as taking the attendance register, reporting to parents and general school administration. In most mainstream school practice, ICT is seen as a tool to be deployed appropriately by professional educators, not as something which will replace them or redefine the fundamental nature of their work.

Some enthusiasts for ICT point to how it increases the potential for pupils to learn on their own, away from school, implying that the work of schools in the future may no longer be based on regular attendance and face to face teaching. While it is true that the quality and availability of distance learning has been increasing steadily over the last 30 years, it is not a new concept. In areas of sparse population, such as the Australian outback or in Alaska, there is a long tradition of distance learning for children for whom school attendance is impractical. In the UK, there has always been a minority of children who are 'educated otherwise than at school' ('EOTAS') for reasons such as long-term hospitalization, school phobia, inability to behave when with other children, pregnancy or because their parents work in travelling fairgrounds and are always on the move. Among adults there is a very long tradition of gaining qualifications by studying through correspondence courses. In all of these cases, there are reasons why conventional face to face teaching and learning with a peer group is impractical. Learning face to face with a peer group in a safe, purpose-designed environment has many educational and social advantages, as well as providing a child-minding service which is important to parents. It is unlikely that many parents and local communities would want to move away from that model as a matter of choice.

The school system fulfils two main purposes. One is helping children to develop skills and understanding, including skills which will be useful in the workplace. The other is helping parents with the upbringing and general well-being of their children, making sure they have the range of experiences appropriate to each stage of their development – development as a whole person, not just as a worker. In this second role, the school is an important part of the infrastructure of a local community. When these two purposes of schooling are considered together in a balanced way, it is difficult to separate the future development of schooling from the future development of the community. For that reason, I see the continuing evolution of schooling as a more likely future scenario than its replacement by something fundamentally different.

Schools operate in the context of their local community but also in two other major contexts. One is, of course, government policies and regulatory systems. The other is the context of professional and academic knowledge about education. The impact of globalization on schooling manifests itself through all three factors (community context, national policy and professional knowledge), and the nature and extent of the impact will occur differentially in relation to each factor according to local circumstances. For a particular school principal wanting to make sense of how 'globalization' is affecting their work, the relevant questions are: 'How is the community my school serves being affected by globalization?', 'In what ways are the policies I am required to implement intended to be responses to globalization?' and 'To what extent does my professional networking and reading give me a global outlook in my work as a school leader?'. The answers to these questions help to map out what 'globalization' means in specific school contexts.

Issues in education

Education systems are constantly changing. Often pressure for change comes from changes in the economic, demographic and technological environments within which education operates. Pressures for change also often arise from changes in society's normative values, beliefs and expectations. These two sets of factors, the environmental and the normative, can change very quickly, whereas educational institutions and regulatory frameworks tend to change more slowly. These factors are summarized in the table below.

	Factors affecting education systems
Normative	Beliefs, values, norms, expectations, aspirations
Institutional	The school system and its regulatory framework, including laws, planning and funding systems, curriculum, assessment and inspection
Environmental	The context of the school system, including characteristics of demographic, economic and technological environments

Often, the current pattern of educational institutions, including the curriculum they teach and the laws that govern them, represent the answer to yesterday's problems, reflecting the environment and values of a previous period. Change in itself is not a problem for educational administrators and policy-makers: the problems arise because related factors change at different speeds.

My conceptual framework for understanding the nature of educational 'problems' is based on a loose adaptation of part of the thinking of Brian Holmes (Holmes, 1965; 1981), (although I reject Holmes's attempts to apply scientific methods to the study of education systems). This suggests that the 'problems' to which changes in the education system are intended to provide 'solutions' can be understood as arising from tensions between and among normative, institutional and environmental factors, in six possible combinations as follows. Of course in real life the six types are often mixed together in complex combinations.

	Causes of issues in education
Type 1	Normative/Normative Conflicting beliefs, aims or values. Examples: tensions between different strands of government policy such as desires for 'excellence' as well as 'inclusion'; 'market forces' as well as 'collaboration'. Also, between liberal attitudes in society, and traditional beliefs of some communities.
Type 2	Normative/Institutional Current aims and aspirations are not met by the current institutions and systems. Example: government's desire for pupils to have wider and earlier experience of vocational education, while schools do not yet have sufficient facilities to provide this.
Type 3	Normative/Environmental Expectations conflict with contextual factors. Example: government places high value on examination grades of a school serving an area of extreme social and economic deprivation with high turnover of pupils.
Type 4	Institutional/Institutional Parts of the institutional and regulatory system are in conflict with each other. Example: government introduced changes to separate the planning and funding of education for pupils over the age of 16 from pre-16 education, but also wanted schools and colleges to offer 14–19 education as a 'coherent phase'.
Type 5	Institutional/Environmental The institutional system is in tension with changing economic, technological and demographic features of the community it serves. Examples: population rising, but not enough school places; or curriculum does not reflect changes in employment market.
Type 6	Environmental/Environmental This pairing of factors is included just for completeness: in practice this will always impact on education as a more complex version of Type 5. Example: area served by the school is suffering reduced social cohesion at the same time as reduced employment prospects.

The history of education policy making in the UK has been dominated by responses to issues of Types 5 and 2. The challenge of providing enough schools and teachers to make education a universal service for an expanding population was, for a long period, a major issue of Type 5. In more recent decades, the challenge of modernizing education to make it more suited to changes in values and in the economy is a major issue of Type 2. The role of governments in relation to these issues has changed. At one time, governments were primarily in the business of solving problems originating in the environment. In more recent times a much more intensive style of government has been adopted which means that governments are now actually one of the main creators of issues of Types 1–5, leading to even more policy initiatives to mitigate their effects.

The changes usually associated with globalization fall mainly in the environmental and normative domains, adding to the new demands that the institutional system struggles to keep pace with. My point in introducing this conceptual framework is to support an argument that the issues for school leaders arising from globalization may appear to be on a larger scale but are not fundamentally different in kind from the other issues with which they are dealing. Indeed, the factor of globalization is inseparable from the issues arising from changes in values, technology, demography or economic conditions, because these changes will often have a global element among their causes.

National policies and politics

The issues arising from related factors changing at different speeds, as outlined above, provide the complex context within which national governments do their work. Dialogue among educationists about education policy can take insufficient account of the realities of political life. It is important to distinguish between policies and politics: that is to say, between the aims and strategies that governments claim to be pursuing, and the motivations and processes that lead to their adoption and affect their implementation.

Benjamin Levin, who has personal experience both as a policy-maker and as an academic analyst, has described the complexities of the political process in terms that reflect completely my own experiences. Levin noted that decisions are shaped by, among other factors, the requirements of staying in office; by symbolic considerations; by limited understanding of situations that are difficult to read; and by a focus on what can be done rather than on what would really make a difference (Levin, 2001: pages 22–23). He considered that 'governments, especially in open political systems, have only limited ability to create the world as they might wish it' (Levin, 2001: page 33). From my experience as a lobbyist I can confirm from an insider perspective the opportunism of some policy developments, notably in relation both to the abolition of the Inner London Education Authority and to the creation of the Office for Standards in Education (Ofsted).

There are other factors that affect the workaday realities of politics. In the UK, governments must appear to be in control because they themselves have cultivated that impression, even in relation to matters where the actual power of decision lies with local government or with individual school governing bodies. When any issue in education becomes newsworthy, journalists will ask, 'What is the government doing about it?', and usually a government spokesperson will wish to give an impression of active involvement. At the same time, the party in power must appear to maintain momentum, and not allow the public to gain an impression that opposition parties are taking control of how issues are debated.

The combined effect of these factors is for governments to launch many 'initiatives' designed to generate publicity; to convey an impression of action; and, through their timing, to upstage the opposition parties. This is why a proportion of government initiatives and announcements turn out, on closer examination, to be vacuous, simply stating in new words policies that have already been agreed. Real policies and developments have to be discerned among the 'noise' of the day to day political process. Public and media expectations of what governments should be achieving to solve every kind of problem are rising, but at the same time there is reduced respect for authority, a breakdown of consensus between government and interest groups, and fragmentation among interest groups.

The popularly held assumption that national government should be held accountable for anything that happens in any classroom has generated risk-averse government. The general public maintains a traditional view of what a school should be like. While governments use the language of innovation and transformation, they do not in practice stray far from tried and tested approaches to educational provision.

In the UK there exist many examples of very radical approaches to school provision, including teaching largely through practical activities; supporting learning in small groups in very informal settings; and teaching mainly through individualized blended learning programmes. The point in common is that these examples are found in special education (for children with learning difficulties and/or disabilities) or in education for children not attending ordinary schools: away from the mainstream and away from the normal focus of attention. In these secluded backwaters innovation has thrived and a more selective attitude has been taken to national policy initiatives. Almost certainly, more radical and innovative practice would develop in mainstream education if governments could find a way to step back and give professional educators more privacy from political attention. That is unlikely to be possible in any general way. The nearest approach to this is likely to be through designated 'innovation zones', where different approaches are tested but where scrutiny will remain high, with an understandable wish not to be seen to be 'experimenting' with children's education.

Local school leadership with a global perspective

Practical political pressures mean that governments must be seen to govern, and it is not realistic to suggest, as Bottery (2004) is inclined to do, that public expressions of education policy should move away from the economic agenda, or that it is possible to 'take politics out of education'. On the other hand, it is equally unrealistic to expect that any modern UK government will be in a position to be a champion of radical educational innovation. The combination of a traditionally minded public, regular elections and the existence of a relentless 'blame culture' means that the most any UK government is likely to do in the direction of genuine educational innovation is to give permission to other agencies, such as individual schools, to develop new approaches to schooling, at their own risk. Even this is likely to be allowed only in the case of schools which have already demonstrated that they are achieving excellence against the normal criteria, and conditional upon those standards being maintained.

I referred earlier to how school leaders have to make a coherent fusion of three sets of demands: the needs and aspirations of their local community; what they know from research and professional practice and government policies. In drawing attention to the balances that have to be struck at local level between these demands, I am not implying that this is a subversive activity. While numerous headteachers that I talk with do portray themselves as having a filtering role, mitigating what they see as potentially adverse impacts of particular national policies, this is in fact a legitimate part of their responsibility. School leaders have a duty, of course, to implement the law. They also have a duty to be competent professionals, and, in the UK, a duty under the general law of education to try as far as possible to educate children in accordance with their parents' wishes, and to safeguard children's well-being. This latter consideration involves school leaders in ethical deliberation about the best interests of the child: a matter explored by Stefkovich and Begley (2007).

There is an enormous gulf between 'top down' and 'bottom up' conceptualizations of education. From the viewpoint of national politicians, the education system is indeed a 'system': a large, albeit complex, organization which can be steered and managed, almost as if the school system had a command and control structure like that found in a multi-national company, with schools as the 'branches' or 'outlets' of a great, united enterprise. From the viewpoint of a parent, 'education' is essentially an individual matter, focused on the development, upbringing and well-being of their child, which involves using the services of a school. While governments emphasize the contribution of schooling to the economy, most children attending school, and their parents, do not pass the day fuelled with the primary motivation that 'My reason for working well in school today is so that in 20 years' time I will contribute to the global competitiveness of British industry'. Their primary concerns and motivations are more personal and more immediate. Perhaps maximizing the extent to which pupils achieve their potential is, after all, the only agenda for schools, and wider concepts such as globalization are only meaningful to the extent that they redefine that potential, and cast new light on the methods by which it may be realized.

The gulf between the concerns and language expressed at different levels leaves a vacuum in school leadership at the local level. School leaders, particularly headteachers acting within a supportive local framework, are the main people who can fill this vacuum. The ways in which school leaders harmonize the demands of national policy, their own professional knowledge and the aspirations of their community represent a major component of local school leadership. Bottery (2007) has researched how headteachers approach that task, their scope for exercising initiative and their perceptions of external constraints. One of his findings was that the wider global dimension was a weak element in this balancing of various demands. Yet each of these three factors has an interface with globalization. My proposition is that the reconciliation of global and local agendas can best occur at the local level through the conscious appraisal of these factors.

An issue to bear in mind is whether, at any particular point of analysis, globalization is to be treated as a dependent or independent variable. Globalization is a dependent variable where the phenomena to which we attach this name are the outcomes of developments occurring in localities and individual nations which have a wider impact. This is globalization as the product of the actions of countries, localities and individuals. In contrast, globalization becomes an independent variable where it is seen as a force with its own momentum which has unavoidable impacts on nations, localities and individuals. This is globalization as a 'top down' process. In fact, the relationship is dynamic, with both of these forces acting concurrently. This means that the populations of localities, and their local school leaders, do not have to be merely the helpless recipients of the impact of globalization, but can instead engage proactively to shape aspects of their future.

Thus the characteristics (and hence educational needs) of the community served by a school will bear some imprint of factors included within the concept of 'globalization': for example, patterns of employment, ethnic composition, and appetite for certain forms of culture and entertainment may be changing. At the same time, that community may itself be having 'globalizing' impacts on other communities, for example through its economic activity, travel and communication patterns.

The professional knowledge drawn upon by school leaders is in a similar dynamic relationship. Modern forms of knowledge exchange give school leaders access to a globalized pool of professional wisdom, at the same time as heightened awareness of local diversity. Many school leaders around the world now straddle two cultures: that of their own national education system and a new culture of international educational conferences, global professional networks, World Bank and OECD perspectives, and the English language literature of school development. Similarly, the frameworks of government policy and regulation within which local school leaders operate are both a response, and contributor, to globalization.

Balancing local and global education priorities requires school leaders to be more consciously aware of these factors and interrelationships, to make sense of them and to translate that understanding into effective leadership. Awareness of the combinations of changing factors that generate issues, illustrated by the six types of issues presented earlier, may help with this sense-making. Reducing tensions between global, national and local priorities also involves identifying which of these tensions are system-generated, and distinguishing tensions of objective fact from tensions which arise from perceptions and language.

Goldspink (2007) suggested a set of principles to guide future education reform. He considered that, to be effective, reform should utilize approaches consistent with the loosely coupled, complex system characteristics of education, rather than approaches based on managerialism or market forces. The principles included drawing on intrinsic motivation, flexibility, risk tolerance, self-organization, institutional learning and a 'non-deficit' approach to reform. These principles would be consistent with more confident and more assertive local system leadership of schooling.

Chris James et al (2007) investigated systemic influences on schools, including a study of primary schools in Wales with high levels of pupil attainment despite socio-economic disadvantage. They explored the notion of 'systemic leadership' encapsulating authorization: conferring authority, endorsing and legitimizing those who lead schools. They rejected a narrow focus on individual school leadership and a narrow focus on school environments which emphasizes challenges, disadvantage or urban characteristics, and current conditions with little attention to history.

James et al saw school systems as wide spatially and historically, concerned not so much with 'change' as with 'authorization'. The successful schools in their study appeared to receive support and 'validation' from the systems within which they worked. They saw this as leadership *for* schools as something wider and different from leadership *of* schools. This implies a policy context for local schools which is supportive, permissive and enabling, and which will give school leaders the confidence and authority to be the champions of educational reform. That can only happen if they, in return, accommodate the political needs of national leaders, which may require the co-construction of new political conceptualizations of local school systems.

12 Independent education: custodian of the past or contributor to the future?

Chris Wright

The independent sector is often seen as routinely conservative. It provides education for some 7 per cent of the school age population in approximately 2,500 schools in the UK. However not only do independent schools provide education for a sizeable minority of children and young people they are often seen by politicians as resources for transforming state education. Here the look is beyond the reactive to issues of their own regenesis and contribution to the wider context of education. This chapter argues that the independent sector has considerable gifts to offer. We will consider the clarity of their vision and ethos building upon tradition and heritage; the child focused holistic view of education; the strength of their pastoral care systems; the value-rich and value-led environments they create; the way in which the market ensures that they are at the cutting edge of educational innovation and their autonomy from central control to create a distinctive education around the needs of the child.

The chapter will draw largely on the work of the independent schools within the Woodard Corporation. The Reverend Canon Nathaniel Woodard (1811–91) was an educational visionary with a passion to transform society by the founding of schools. These schools were to be more than instruments of academic education. They were to be strong collegiate communities, a form of religious enterprise as dedicated to forming moral taste and character as to delivering a formal curriculum. Nathaniel Woodard had a concern for the well-being of society. He lived at a time of social conflict. All agreed that provision for middle-class education was insufficient. Within his life time he founded 11 schools. Today Woodard Schools meet the needs of pupils from all sections of society. The Woodard Corporation is a unique family of schools comprising 22 owned independent schools, five independent associated schools and 13 state-maintained schools, with three schools abroad (in Malawi, Tennessee and Brisbane). In September 2009 they will open their first two Academies.

Vision, ethos and leadership

Independent schools stand out from each other. They have to in order to survive in the current competitive economic climate. Ipso Mori (2008) concludes that they are some of the most popular schools around today. Parents recommend their clear vision and ethos, strong discipline policy and the excellence of provision. As the Provost of Woodard comments, 'Our schools have taught us the importance of developing traditions that embody the story of the school, so that pupils are inducted into the realm of meaning through symbol and ceremony. While today some of these ceremonies (e.g., 'Jerusalem Heights' at Abbots Bromley School for Girls) may appear antiquated they still provide pupils with a strong feeling of identity and loyalty'.

This vision is founded on a clearly articulated and owned philosophy of education that is often broader and more explicit than that in the state-maintained sector which is often constrained by its sometimes singular focus on academic achievements and standards. Nathaniel Woodard's offering of Christian spirituality in schools is as much to do with formation and vocation as it is to do with academic entitlement. It is focused on personal growth. That is why in our schools the government's Every Child Matters agenda has always been the backbone of all that they do. Woodard schools are founded on the following intentions (2009):

- Help young people develop character – people with largeness of soul and personal dignity and integrity.
- Encourage students to become active, compassionate, inquiring and life-long learners, in search of truth.
- Nurture creativity and capacity for independent and critical thought.
- Help young people develop a positive self-awareness and self-confidence.
- Develop internationally minded young people who, recognizing their common humanity and shared guardianship of the planet, help to create a better and more peaceful world through intercultural understanding and respect.

Everyone included, every challenged, everyone successful

In recent years the government has introduced the child-centred concept of personalization. Independent schools have taken it for granted that each child should be personally known, loved and nurtured in all that they do. This approach is encapsulated in many of the mission statements of independent schools. For example:

> We are concerned to encourage individuals to achieve their very best. We provide many opportunities for everyone to develop their talents and discover their strengths. (St Margaret's School, Exeter)

We genuinely offer our boys and girls an education for life. We passionately believe that all our pupils must be given every opportunity to achieve the best possible grades so that they can progress…we also work hard to foster the life-long love of learning so essential if they are to thrive in an increasingly competitive and rapidly changing world. As importantly, we aim to develop those skills and qualities which will turn such paper qualifications into success, and also help to promote happiness in later life. (Hurstpierpoint College, West Sussex)

In common with most independent schools, Woodard schools have always regarded intelligence or talent as multi-faceted. They act on the belief that all pupils (not some or the many) can succeed. The skill is in identifying the particular talents of each child and working with each child individually to develop their potential. At Hurstpierpoint College each pupil is measured against their own potential and not against the potential of someone else. For example, all can belong to a sports team and take their part in fixtures. There is an educational entitlement that goes far beyond that defined by academic outcomes. Each pupil is entitled to be applauded on stage for an accomplishment, to take part in a sports fixture and to perform on a stage. The curriculum offering is broad enough to allow this to happen, and to ensure that each individual pupil's talent is spotted and nurtured.

The following snapshot of a weekend's activities at Ardingly College, West Sussex, recorded through its newsletter (2009), could be replicated in many of our schools:

Again it has been a wonderful term, I think summed up on the weekend of Saturday 14 and Sunday 15 March, when we had a full raft of activities for the students to engage in, including a full hockey fixture list against Seaford College; netball against Roedean; a Cabaret night for the boys, girls and parents; our Rugby Sevens team participating in the Llandovery Under 15 Invitation Sevens; our Under 18 boys playing in the Worth Sevens; our girls' Under 18 netball team went to the Marlborough Tournament and came 5th out of 27 schools; and to top off the Sunday evening we had an outstanding performance as part of Music @ Ardingly series, by the Royal String Quartet. We even had a Maths Detention on the Sunday, so it wasn't all play!'

With their focus on developing every facet of individual talent it is no surprise that the success of their students in sporting, artistic and cultural fields far outweighs numbers. For example, former independent school pupils won 32.7 per cent of Britain's medals in the 2004 Olympics and 37.3 per cent in the 2008 Olympics (Smithers and Robinson, 2008). Their success in personalizing education and developing all forms of talent could provide state schools with the confidence to move away from the constraints of valuing what they measure to measuring what they value, and embedding the ECM agenda in all that they do. The best independent schools have developed intelligent uses of data to measure what they value. They have audited individual personal profiles of each student. In the past it might have been the case that students in independent schools had to fit in with the culture of the institution. The institution came first. However, today independent schools have often led the way in focusing on the needs of each individual child and forming and developing each of them individually.

Every child known, loved and nurtured

That every child is individually known, loved and nurtured has led to independent schools often being at the forefront of innovative pastoral care systems. For example, at Ardingly College students are able to select their own tutor. The tutor has the responsibility of meeting one to one with each of their tutees for a minimum of half an hour every two weeks. Tutors are expected to support the student in all aspects of their lives, including attending sporting fixtures, drama productions, informal concerts, etc. irrespective of whether the student is a boarding or day student. The head of Ardingly College, Peter Green, commented in an interview given in May 2009, 'Children will always notice when you are there – they feel supported and cared for.' The tutor has a transformational role in inspiring, supporting and challenging their tutees. In this way no child is lost in the system. This personal commitment to the individual child stands in stark contrast to the role of the form tutor in some of the state-maintained schools, a role that is down-skilled into administrative tasks or, at best, the delivery of a PSHE programme.

Boarding provision adds an enriched dimension to many of our independent schools and teaches our students what it means to live within a community. They lead the way and embody what many of our state schools aspire to in their concept of the 'extended school'. In establishing boarding schools Nathaniel Woodard was attempting to meet the needs of the fragmented society he saw around him. In many ways they stand in polar contrast with much of modern day nuclear society, where people do not easily mix with each other.

> By the time a child reaches the Upper Sixth we know them better than their parents. We see them when they are happy and when they are sad. We are one community in which students of all ages mix together within their 'House'. Living and working in a boarding community enables us all to learn skills and aptitudes essential for living a successful life: we learn the importance of duty as an essential part of belonging and a corollary to the concept of rights: duty as loyalty, purpose and caring for others.' (Peter Green interview, May 2009)

Value-rich and value-driven

One of the reasons that independent schools are so popular with parents is that they are value-rich and value-driven communities. Independent schools have often been custodians promoting timeless values. For example, the following 'Values Statement' from Queen Mary's School, Thirsk is very explicit on its stance about absolute values – a stark contrast to some of the more relativistic statements one finds in many schools:

We believe that truth, justice and goodness exist absolutely…We emphasize that it is the ability and willingness to seek for truth and to judge our own actions against an absolute standard that makes each of us human. We teach that each child needs to pursue the spiritual dimension in order to be able to live a fulfilled life. In particular she must learn to avoid those actions which diminish her as a human being and seek to do those things which make her more fully human. (Queen Mary's Thirsk Values Statement 2009)

The role of the school as stewards of values is underlined by the very fact that in Woodard schools the chair of the governing body is called the 'custos'. 'We ensure that the nature and ethos of the school is something that is very clear to everyone' says Robert Alston, Custos of Ardingly College (Interview with author, June 2009). Woodard schools provide a strong and distinctive vision and ethos based on Christian beliefs and values. They actively teach the importance of the value of love, forgiveness, truthfulness, integrity, courage, generosity and respect to all people. They believe that education is much more than a 'service industry'. At its best it should have a prophetic voice and should work to change the world for the better, to pursue peace and justice. This passion arises out of Nathaniel Woodard's vision of education as a transformative change agent in society.

At the leading edge of education

As a result of independent schools needing to anticipate and respond to pupil and parents' needs they have often been pioneers of educational innovation. This is the certainly the case of the founders of many of the independent schools. While Nathaniel Woodard could not be considered as a radical in relation to curriculum design, he moved away from complete allegiance to the traditional classical model of education and introduced a whole range of vocational courses to meet the needs of the pupils in his care. In 1850 Woodard founded a Military and Engineering school, a precursor of the Diploma programme. He had the foresight to establish a teacher training school for 'Commercial Schoolmasters' (Heeney, 1969: pages 28 and 33). In 1860 Hurstpierpoint College was one of the first schools to have a cadet force. It also offered a wide range of academic courses, including boys studying technical and military subjects for the Indian Civil Service examinations. In the twentieth century it was one of the first schools running a Challenge of Industry course for Sixth Formers, who undertook shadowing with senior executives.

Today this pioneering spirit continues. For example, one of our Preparatory Schools, King's Hall in Taunton, was one of the first schools to open a Forest School. Set in superb woodland grounds, their Forest School is at the very heart of the Early Years education. The outdoor environment is one of the best classrooms for developing the students' independence, self-esteem and problem-solving skills as well as providing a wealth of activities that encourage pupils to learn together and as part of a team. Today, the Headmaster of Hurstpierpoint College sits on the governing body of Littlehampton Academy as they work to design a vocational street open to the community at the heart of the Academy, and the Headmaster of Lancing College sits on the newly formed governing body of the Sir Robert Woodard Academy in West Sussex as they extend their performing arts specialist status in developing a mini Barbican suite. As Peter Green, Headmaster of Ardingly College says:

> Because we are independent we have a responsibility to be innovative, to always seek improvement. We always ask ourselves how we can be a market leader, and provide the very best education we can for each individual child. It is this innovative edge that nearly ten years ago caused us to enrich our sixth form offer and provide the International Baccalaureate Diploma alongside the more traditional A-level route. Currently we are reviewing our Key Stage 4 offer based on creating a profile of a young person equipped to take on the world. This means radically rethinking what education is for, and reducing the number of GCSE qualifications our pupils take in order to introduce a greater enrichment programme. These include extended projects in order to develop research techniques as well as a raft of coaching qualifications for Year 11. (ibid)

Outreach to the community

Independent schools offer the educational establishment a wide vision of their role in society. They are often collegiate communities that look outwards by offering educational opportunities to a wide group of people, including partnerships with state schools. This is especially so within the Woodard Corporation where independent and state schools have a history of working collaboratively to share good and improving practice. Each year students, chaplains, governors, teachers and headteachers come together from across all sectors to learn together and share best practice on student leadership (Prefects' Course held in one of our schools), Sixth Form Oxbridge Masterclasses (held in Trinity College, Oxford), Governors' Training, Chaplains' and Headteachers' Conferences (to share best leadership practice).

Independent schools offer a rich diversity of outreach programmes to the local, national and global community. For example, from its earliest days Lancing College led a mission to Camberwell, East London, resulting in the provision of full Sixth Form scholarships that still exists to this day. Typical of the benefits of this collegiality is the story of David Quarty who came from Camberwell to Hurstpierpoint College on a boarding scholarship, and then went on to become Head Boy of Lancing College. Today he has returned to the successor school of Archbishop Michael Ramsey School in Camberwell, namely St Michael & All Angel's Academy as a teacher to give back in service what he has benefited.

Individual independent schools have developed high levels of expertise in specific areas of the curriculum that they share with the larger community. For example, Ellesmere College promotes sporting excellence and have established a joint school and community elite swimming club in Shropshire that provides children aged eight and upwards with one to one coaching, enabling them to compete at a national level in galas. Many independent schools have cooperated with state schools as part of the Independent State School Partnerships grants scheme introduced in 1998. For example, the 'Building Bridges' partnership between King's School, Tynemouth and their local 11–16 school, focuses on developing modern foreign languages and provides for the teaching of Russian. But this is just one among many examples that could be quoted. The following extract from Peterborough High School's magazine about their annual Science Day, to which they invite local state primary school students, gives a flavour of the resources and subject expertise that many independent schools share with others:

> The Quantum Theatre provided an energetic and factual show on 'Quirk in the work'; looking at the topic of electricity in a comical presentation combining song, dance and strange goings-on with electricity...Year 5 built mini classroom rockets out of simple household materials. We had a room of flying rockets within minutes of the water being added...Year 6 became forensic scientists to help solve a crime. They looked at fingerprints, compared different fibres under the microscope, investigated a suspicious alibi and analysed soil samples. In the end they gathered enough evidence to firmly place 'Fingers Ratchford' at the scene of the crime. Demonstrating excellent laboratory skills, Year 3 pupils investigated the presence of enzymes in different foods. Using the idea of catalytic converters in cars to introduce the concept of natural catalysts, the pupils carefully measured hydrogen peroxide into boiling tubes, cut up samples of food and collected oxygen gas. (Peterborough High School Magazine, 2009)

The influence of independent schools on education extends well beyond their walls. Public service has always been a part of the independent school ethos. Far from being factories for the production of academic qualifications, our independent schools have been outward looking. They have strong international links, often begun through service and mission. For example, Lancing College have created links with St Anne's Hospital in Malawi and so far have used their fundraising campaign to carry out substantial building projects including a guardian shelter (1998), staff housing (2002), a male surgical ward (2006) and a ward for TB patients (2008). Students visit Malawi on a biannual basis to help in the painting and decoration of the hospital. Worksop College has developed an educational exchange programme with Kipsigak High School in Kenya that enables senior leaders and teachers to share best pedagogic practice, as well as financially supporting individual students to attend school and take part in joint school expeditions.

The government recognizes that independent schools are an important catalyst for improvement in the state sector. Lord Andrew Adonis summarized it when he said 'it is your educational DNA we are seeking' (2007). A growing number of independent schools have become lead sponsors in the government's academy programme. Woodard Schools is the lead sponsor of two Academies on the West Sussex coast. Each Academy replaces an existing school, both of which lie at the bottom of the county's league tables for academic performance. In keeping with our founder's aim to extend and promote education each of the Academies will inherit the DNA of the Woodard Corporation, ensuring that each child is known, loved and nurtured. Each Academy will be divided into a number of smaller schools called chapters, very much after, but more than, the independent school house system, thus ensuring that each child has a strong sense of belonging and identity. These chapters will focus on developing all aspects of the pupil and show a deep commitment to character formation and excellence, an emphasis on the importance of living out clearly articulated values and a passion to make a positive difference in the world. The Academies are also learning from some of the innovative curriculum designs of our independent school. For example, Littlehampton Academy is redesigning its Year 9 creative arts curriculum around the AQA Baccalaureate courses after hearing them profiled by independent school colleagues at their recent headteachers conference. It is also worthy of note that there is an emerging trend for independent school heads to become the principals of Academies.

Independence

The very independence of these schools is one contributor to their success, according to a recent research report into independent schools by Smithers and Johnson (2008) through Buckingham University: 'Headteachers of independent schools saw themselves as having the freedom to do what is right for the pupils rather than having to continually comply with externally imposed initiatives'. This is especially the case in the freedom they have to tailor the curriculum to meet all pupils' needs, and to make decisions faster and be more effective. This compares favourably with the state-maintained sector, where schools can feel oppressed by the continual stream of government initiatives. Consider this comment from a teacher in a state school: 'State education has become a factory farm. Every day it has been like going into some very big impersonal factory and it is like you are a cog in it.' (ibid).

The government has recognized the importance of school autonomy in its Academies programme. Sponsors and Academy principals have a mandate to regenerate schools with a powerful vision of what education is about, to instil a clearly defined ethos into all that the Academy does, and then to use all the flexibility that its independence gives to meet the needs of the pupils: be it in changing the pattern of the school day or year, its organization into horizontal or vertical groups, the quality of its pastoral care, its commitment to outreach into, and inclusion of, the wider community, not to mention transforming the pedagogy. However, many sponsors are starting to discover that some of the Academy's independence is being stripped away. They still lack the key freedom of fully independent schools which have to anticipate and respond to parent and pupil needs through the market rather than having to take direction from central government.

Summary

Nathaniel Woodard established some of the most innovative and prophetic educational institutions of their day. While today the independent sector is often seen as routinely conservative, I have argued that they hold within them the catalyst for the regeneration of the wider educational scene. The gifts they bring include: their custody of a clear vision of the ends of education, their independence and autonomy to provide education at the point of a pupil's needs and in quick response to market forces, their confidence to do what is right and not to be dictated to from above and their commitment to holistic education, developing individual abilities to the full and the formation of the child. Through sharing expertise and facilities their influence on education is growing, both in this country and through the world.

Part 3
THE CHANGING CLASSROOM

13 Neuroscience, education and the decline of self-deception

Will Thomas

This chapter begins with a review of the impact of neuroscience on learning and ends with a global vision for education. It moves from the analytical to the holistic. I hope that it provokes you and touches you. Above all, I hope that it calls you to action.

Where are we now? Collective guilt

During his life between 1875 and 1961 Carl Jung, influential psychologist and father of modern psychotherapy, developed his concept of collective unconsciousness. Jung suggested that there was an innate repository of cultural experience and common ancestral heritage which all humankind could access. Speculation regarding the nature of this unconsciousness continues to this day. Whether it is psychological, genetic, transmitted by folklore, or indeed folklore in its own right remains open to debate. Using this idea can cause it to grow in your psyche and you start to notice it around you. Do you ever tap into the collective unconscious among members of your profession? This pervasive cognition appears in the form of beliefs and sayings, and can often surface emotionally. Have you ever noticed the cloud of collective guilt that appears when educationalists talk of their craft? Some remark 'I never know when I have done enough' or 'I am not sure whether the approach I am taking is the right one' and 'I'm in constant doubt as to whether I am doing the best by students'. I would suggest that this collective guilt, exacerbated by the relentless drive to improve attainment for learners and performance among teachers, has created an almost fanatical need to find definitive answers to big learning questions like:

1 What are the best approaches to teaching to maximize learning?
2 How do we learn?
3 How can we engage and fulfil learners?
4 How do we know if we are maximizing the potential of learners?

Over the last 20 years popular, scientific, pseudo-scientific, sociological and psychological theories have been offered in answering these questions. They have been variously packaged as fads, initiatives, cycles, lunch-packs and toolkits. In the last 15 years one of the most persistent models of developing learning and teaching in education has been so-called 'Brain-based Learning'. It rests on the growth of research into the structural and functional organization of the brain.

Progressively sophisticated investigative techniques including electron-microscopy, electro-encephalograms (EEG) and functional magnetic resonance imaging (fMRI) have revealed detailed data about how the brain is built and operates. On many levels we are now more aware of the brain's mysteries than ever before. But just how useful is this data when it comes to interpreting the implications for the classroom?

Beware the generalizations

In straw-polls I conducted in some recent teacher training, 86 per cent of teachers questioned believed that understanding how the brain worked was 'very important' to teaching and learning. Of the remaining 14 per cent, only 3 per cent thought brain research was unimportant. But are they right to be so convinced of its usefulness? A report published in 2007 by The Teaching and Learning Research Programme and backed by The Economic and Social Research Council urges caution in the way we apply brain research to classroom settings. It asserts that 'brain research does not give rise to lesson plans', and warns of the inflexibility of the research equipment, i.e. fMRI scanning techniques tell us little about young people's brains as most research is done on adults. Additionally it tells us little about the complexities of learning in the classroom context. In an important balancing act, the report goes on to guard against rejecting neuroscience altogether, suggesting instead that we keep an open mind. In this same report Dr Liane Kaufmann of Innsbruck University Children's Hospital says of neuroscience and its usefulness in classrooms: '....there's still a long way to go. Nevertheless, I'm convinced a better understanding of the neural underpinnings of behaviour and learning will not only enhance our knowledge of how the brain-behaviour relationship develops, but will also help tailor pedagogical curricula'. (page 22)

Neuroscience has already supported our understanding. It has caused us to re-evaluate theories of thought processing, like hemispheric lateralization. We have discovered that older notions of analytical thinking taking place in the left hemisphere and holistic thinking in the right brain hemisphere are over simplistic. We have also learned a good deal about specific conditions such as dyslexia and ADHD. Some useful support strategies have emerged from this. We more fully understand the effects of dehydration, sleep deprivation and caffeine use on the brain. In each case, however, the leap from clinic to classroom is still speculative.

Pop-psychology and the mythology of brain research

Approaches popularized in the early part of this decade, such as Accelerated Learning (AL), drew on generalized applications of brain research in such areas as hydration, sleep, colour therapy and energizing techniques such as 'brain breaks'. Even advocates of these approaches in the 90s and Noughties now admit that some of the leaps from laboratory to learner were highly generalized. Approaches such as 'brain breaks', which have popularized lateral movement exercises to re-energize learners and improve thinking, may have been 'over-scienced'. I visit schools and talk to educators regularly. Numerous success stories emerge of re-engaged learners, of significant breakthroughs for young people through brain-based approaches that work. So while the claimed science behind some of these approaches might not be robust and the outcomes are often not formally measured, there is case study evidence for their effectiveness.

My conclusion is that underneath many of the popular brain-based learning approaches including Accelerated Learning, there would seem to be a range of workable psychological models of learning. For example, at its core, AL has a learning cycle which is based on an established learning platform, namely Kolb's Experiential Learning Model (1984). It could be argued that the psychological models of learning and behaviour which have been around for much longer than neuroscience and are based on observation of practice still offer us the best frameworks for planning for learning. I would therefore argue that these approaches, while they may offer somewhat over-egged scientific claims, do provide robust learning models which work in practice. Neuroscience is sometimes providing evidence to validate them at a physiological level. I have personally seen thousands of teachers and hundreds of organizations enable significant and positive improvements for their learners through using so called 'brain-based' approaches. The evidence of efficacy for many is a high level of enthusiasm among learners and teachers and improvements in climate and attainment. Sadly this collective perceived success is not measured and recorded in ways in which would pass statistical scrutiny. There is a balance to be struck between logic and instinct. We can place too much emphasis on measurement and dismiss that which is not easily measurable nor research funded.

The lack of applicability to classroom practice of much neuroscience remains a challenge to its use. It does however have great promise and potential to underpin many of the observation-based psychological models that teachers find immediately useful. There will always be a paradox between clinical research and the daily experience of teachers.

My suggestion for the future is that the profession develops an embedded Global-Local Integration Approach (GLIA). GLIA, put simply, would be a system of channelling research from scientific study directly into schools. Within those institutions educators will be actively engaged in action research that locates clinical research into the classroom and experiments with it at the local level. This GLIA will be actualized by groups of educators meeting regularly and co-coaching, dialoguing, challenging and recording practice. Centrally located, the outcomes of GLIA are published for all to access, providing a 'collective conscious' within organizations that is highly pertinent to their setting.

Education on purpose

What we have explored so far is current and perhaps GLIA could work in your school already or even be grown organically over the coming years. What I would like to explore next is more far reaching. Probably the most important question educators need to answer and stay connected to is: What is the purpose of education?

If you are an educator or close to the profession, you'll know the nagging doubts that creep in about the hefty content needing to be delivered and the lack of opportunity for learners to learn experientially. In this section of the chapter I intend to present a provoking global perspective on education for the next few hundred years. This is a vision that is focused on *purpose* and *values*, foundations that can become lost in the pressure to deliver.

The future. New education – old values

We live in challenging times. We are approaching the end of an era of plenty. We have plundered the planet. The end of the world is nigh! These are perhaps familiar statements in the media, on billboards and sandwich boards in a town near you. We can push them into our blind spot and dismiss them as the statements of doom-mongers and cranks, or we can look at them and consider the truths they speak. Any future education planning must surely continue to meet the needs of the nation, but I would strongly assert that they should now explicitly embrace the needs of our wider global community.

Education in the UK has been for a long time focused on feeding an economic growth model, providing suitable workers for the utopian promise of continuing economic growth, which works on the questionable premise that a rising tide benefits all boats.

Recently, we have seen a catastrophic meltdown of the financial system. All of us were surprised at the scale of the crash. Anti-globalizationists herald the breakdown of the Anglo-American capitalist model of society. In recent decades our economy has increasingly moved away from manufacturing and towards more invisible and intangible earnings in the form of financial industry and service-based products. How can we have had a period of sustained economic growth and yet be so debt-ridden, individually and nationally? This must surely be the time to ask questions, not just of our fiscal system, but our growth-based presuppositions.

It has become difficult to ignore the rising tide of evidence that our planet is under duress. While arguably the planet itself and life in most forms will survive the rape of its resources, civilization may not. However you look at the evidence for global warming, resource depletion, population growth and competition for resources, we are in trouble in the longer term. Catastrophizers don't help, but plain logic tells us that life as we know it cannot continue, given the exponentially increasing pressures on resources over the next few hundred years. What will our children's children's children say about us, as we sat by and watched humankind implode?

I would suggest that there are three globally significant challenges facing the biosphere over the next few hundred years:

1   Competition for increasingly scarce resources exacerbated by population growth and global warming
2   Human values conflicts
3   Social inequality

The likelihood is that these three factors will have combined effects, which will change our way of life considerably. Global warming, on its own, creating rising sea levels, is likely to cause increased competition for energy, land, water and food, displacing great numbers of people. Conflicts of values between peoples and nations will be exacerbated by the scarcity of resources. Social inequality will be heightened by the nomadic existence of large numbers of people. Conflict will very likely become more prevalent than even today.

Arguably, driving this outcome is the very philosophy which has brought us to the 2008/9 economic meltdown. The utopia of continued economic growth is coming up against a growing realization that resources are finite, and using those resources has significant, gradual and cumulative effects on populations.

While as educators we might be carrying guilt about doing the best in our classrooms, there is another guilt that we carry. This emotion is internal conflict surrounding our affluent Western life styles. Some of us locate this guilt in a blind spot somewhere out of view. That collective guilt surrounds the global social inequity that is necessary, so that we can continue to enjoy our lifestyles. The ignored responsibility that underlies *this* wider collective guilt is one that needs, I would suggest, to be addressed within the purpose of our education system for the future.

The education system of the future must provide for skill development so that learners can become independent, as it has always done, but much more than this, it will need to prepare learners to cooperate, to compromise, to find common ground rather than difference, to embrace the global family of humankind, and to focus on needs not wants; to be satisfied with less materially and in so doing gain more in well-being. This will involve education which concentrates on awareness-raising of self and others. It will need to prepare learners to build their self-esteem based on character and kindness, not material possessions and status. It will need to enable them to recognize the insidious marketing machine that seeks to knock them from their confidence and aims to breed the necessary self-doubt that advertisers must generate in order to make sales. It needs to enable them to make informed choices about this subliminal barrage. The new education will focus our kids on building independence and interdependence, cooperation and the actualization of themselves and others. It will need to be a system that encourages young people to embrace Fromm's notion of 'being' rather than 'having'; in other words, becoming satisfied through giving and sharing, as opposed to the short-lived 'hits' of possession, competition and acquisition. It will need to mobilize them to challenge the powerful forces that will seek self gratification and ego-fulfilment.

This education will focus on the *process* of learning, rather than swathes of imminently outdated content. It will promote interdependent thinking and problem-solving. Let's build a new education for this millennium based not on short-sighted economic targets, but on far-sighted ideas of how we want the world to be for our children's children's children.

A manifesto for a new education:

- Awareness of self and others
- A system based on collaboration not competition
- Finding common ground, celebrating diversity and resolving conflict
- Access to relevant and enriching learning for all.
- An understanding of custodianship of the earth's resources
- Connection to, and respect for, the wonder of the natural world
- The challenging of behaviours that threaten the lives of fellow human beings
- Actively working towards living simple lives, based on needs not wants
- Service to the wider community of life

As you look at this list you may ask whether the solutions to our challenges lie not in some technological future, but in the simplicity of the past. That the values and practices that have sustained humankind over thousands of years, and which seem to have been thrown away in the last century, might well come to serve us once more. Equally, just as the UK, Europe and America have become the model of progress, so that pendulum may well swing back to the East to the ancient cultures, philosophies and practices of yesteryear.

In Bhutan there is a measure of national progress known Gross Domestic Happiness. It is used to assess levels of national well-being. There is evidence that the people of Bhutan, while having very little materially, are contented on the whole. We could take a lead from this, not just at an educational level but also at a political level.

I believe passionately that it is only through knowing ourselves and through questioning our actions and motivations that we can truly serve ourselves and others. In sympathy with Bhutan, I would suggest a new measure for the West, that of Gross Domestic Awareness, and that we develop an Awareness Economy. The Awareness Economy would be based on driving up levels of self-knowledge and responsibility for your own actions towards yourself and others. This Awareness Economy would thrive on the eradication of blind spots that allow us to perpetuate inequality and it would promote stillness of mind as a desirable outcome.

The new education must encourage self-reflection and must encompass the values of Fromm's 'being' orientation. The 'Century of Selfishness' is over. The 'Century of Self-Awareness' is here. It's time to begin the new centuries of Global Collaboration.

It's time to accept and embrace neuroscience, computer technology and all the other threads of discovery. Let's use them, let's make them work for us, but for goodness sake let's know why we're using them and what's really important. Let us operate from a set of values that supports rather than exploits. Let's teach our children to be altruists not egotists. Let's ensure that what we head towards is a future that will leave our own consciences and the collective unconscious of humankind free of guilt.

I am not a professor, nor a doctor, nor an economist. I am a member of the human race who cares passionately about people and about our ecosystem. You might say this vision I outline is all just pie in the sky. But that could just be your mechanism for pushing this back into your blind spot. If, as a result of reading this, you wake up to something you have been hiding away and, crucially, take some action, then you immediately begin to put the vision to work. You become part of the solution.

Ghandi said 'Be the change you want to see in the world'. That is our challenge…it's up to all of us each day…so what will you be contributing to the collective unconscious this week? How will you *be part of the change*?

(With grateful thanks to: Richard King, Nicky Anastasiou, Penny Clayton, Sarah Mook, Tom Hill, Brin Best, William Bloom, Angus McLeod.)

14 Rousseau revisited: formal and personal education

John Eaton

'It takes a village to raise a child'

African proverb

Introduction

In this chapter I want to argue that if formal education is not complemented by methods that elicit social and emotional intelligence from the child then a variety of problems will result that may mean that formal education never gets started. And should it get started it may never be completed if the child does not know how to make use of the 'learning' she has been offered. And that even if it is 'finished' it may make little difference to her quality of life.

A case example

This case is my own and in describing it I hope to make clear my purpose in bringing this issue before the reader of this chapter.

I possess a PhD in Psychology, a Masters in Psychotherapy and a BA in Philosophy. I have lectured in these matters at every grade from A level through to professional seminars and up to university undergraduate level. An educational success? Perhaps so. And yet I left school at 15.

After a long period of poor behaviour, indiscipline and dire exam grades at the grammar school I attended in the UK during the 1970s, my teachers made it clear to me that there was little point in my continuing and, that if I did, I would very soon be expelled. My working-class father was delighted. He saw formal education as a pointless diversion from the real business of learning a trade and making money. So he found me an apprenticeship and it was another four (wasted) years before I found the courage to go back into education on another footing.

Although the potential for academic achievement at the grammar school was present, in my case it was vitiated by immaturity in social relations and self-management; a defect that may have been remediable.

My key difficulty was that I was often overcome by inchoate states of frustration, despondency and rage. These states were hard for me to name, let alone identify. They typically came up after I had been bullied or punished for what I saw as minor offences, or ridiculed by a teacher, or sitting through lessons in subjects for which I had little interest.

Looking back, I can see clearly that my bad behaviour was promoted by rebelliousness, attention-seeking and revenge. Naturally these responses merely compounded the problem and set the scene for more interactional problems. Another key problem was that the school: its rules, its ethos, and its teaching style seemed both alien and nonsensical to me. Partly this was due to my being one of the very few working-class children at the school. But, more profoundly, I lacked an enlightened tutor – or mentor – who could 'interpret' for me. I really needed to be taught how to work the system as well as to recognize both the sources of, and the solution to, my own despair.

What is formal learning?

What I mean by 'formal learning' is that it proceeds by reading off, analyzing and representing the ideas and rules and applying within a particular intellectual domain. Those rules may be inherent in the subject matter (e.g., the laws of physics), the organization of the subject (e.g. the relation of geology and weather patterns to geography), or the interpretations of older writers (e.g. Chaucer or Gibbon). A formal education certifies whether or not a student is able to identify, understand and re-argue the rules of the domain under scrutiny.

Since at least the fifteenth century education in the West has been singularly biased towards this type of intellectual training. Indeed, it was the grammar schools, first founded in medieval times, that were its starting point. Their sole initial function was to provide tuition in Latin grammar. That would enable their pupils to acquire an education through a reading of Greek and Roman historians, philosophers, poets, dramatists and natural scientists. Later, by extension, the grammar schools undertook the tuition of literature, natural science, history, geography, mathematics and other subjects. It was expected that this would constitute the education of a gentleman, preparing him for university entrance or (more probably) a career at court, in the law, in parliament, or in the church. This humanistic scheme was later on supplemented by education in the physical sciences and, later still, by education in such subjects as economics, psychology and sociology. Still later, women were deemed worthy of formal education and were granted access to these riches.

The education of a citizen

During the eighteenth century formal learning was subjected to a critique by Jean-Jacques Rousseau in his didactic novel, *Emile*, in which he argued that a complete education also attended to the emotional and social interests of the person.[1] There is too little space here to describe Rousseau's theory in detail but here are a number of key points from *Emile* relevant to this chapter:

1 Unless we cultivate self-love in the child (*amour-de-soi* – what we nowadays might call 'self-esteem') he[2] will not become socially mature.

2 If children possess *amour-de-soi* they will express their natural hunger to learn and mature.

3 For Rousseau the intellectual development of a human being proceeds in stages, from habits, to sensory and physical interests, to emotional give and take, and then on to rational inquiry. There is little point in foisting formal education on a child until he is able to make use of it.

4 Learning how to express and cultivate the emotions (Rousseau: 'the passions') is a crucial prerequisite for intellectual development. Without them the child will not have a reason to undergo the hard work of study. Nor will he be able to form good relationships with his tutors or relate his acquired knowledge to the demands of society.

5 If the student is truly to own his learning for himself he must acquire it not via rote but through personal experiment, debates with authority and, with the use of his reasoning skills, reach his own conclusions.

6 The final aim of education is the full expression of the individual's capacity for love, virtue, citizenship and rational enquiry.

7 The adolescent's formal education should unfold side by side with a gradual entry into communal life. As the youth becomes a citizen his intellectual training fosters his desire for the good life, and vice versa.

8 Practical education supplements formal education as the youth understands that his thoughts, desires and actions have consequences – both in the abstract and through personal experience.

9 Education can never be impersonal; educational methods must be tailored to the individual.

10 Education can never be an end in itself. Its purpose is the creation of happy, virtuous and complete human beings.

Rousseau, like many of his contemporaries, was consciously harking back to classical ideals. Specifically to the Greek notion of *Paideia* (Jaeger, 1945), in which the aim of education was principally the cultivation of the complete man: well read, sensitive, virtuous, artistic, athletic, and a good soldier and citizen.

Rousseau is a historical example of one writer who argued – influentially –for the basic view that I am propounding here: that both personal and formal learning are co-necessities. Others include Plato, John Locke, Humboldt and Dewey (see Curren,

2006 for a review). More recently, Howard Gardner has widened the debate by calling attention to the existence of multiple intelligences, the majority of which, despite their importance, are not developed in formal learning programmes. In the next section I want to focus on two of these: interpersonal and intrapersonal intelligence and describe how they are relevant to personal learning.

The education we did not receive

In his seminal work on multiple intelligences *Frames of Mind* (1993), Gardner delineates eight types of intelligence, of which only two – linguistic and logico-mathematical intelligence – are relevant to formal learning as traditionally conceived. Two others – intrapersonal and interpersonal intelligence[3] – are crucial to the development of personal learning.

Intrapersonal intelligence. The ability to read off one's bodily sensations, feeling and emotions, link these to the situation one is in and take appropriate action on these emotional prompts. This type of intelligence implies that the person can link actions to consequences, take adaptive action and accumulate a steadily growing repertoire of subtly distinct behaviours that get results.

Interpersonal intelligence. The ability to recognize and interpret the emotions, motivations and intentions of other people, relate one's observations to the situation that person is in and respond appropriately. This type of intelligence implies basic acquired traits such as empathy and social communication (Eaton and Johnson, 2001).

Until recently both kinds of intelligence have been overlooked in standard Western educational curricula. A landmark was the 2001 White Paper published by the UK government, *Schools Achieving Success*, which enunciated a new policy of 'strengthening the emotional intelligence of pupils' on the grounds that this would both improve behaviour in secondary schools and would raise the level of academic achievement. It would be fair to say, however, that the application of this policy has so far been patchy, with only a few trials seen in UK educational authorities so far. Even so, *The Times* reported in 2005 that one programme that taught primary school children how to recognize and express emotions, develop 'good manners' and respect for others resulted in reduced truancy rates, fewer exclusions, a drop in 'serious behaviour incidents' and improvements in English and Maths grades.

Standard emotional intelligence programmes develop both intrapersonal and interpersonal intelligence in a variety of ways:

Intrapersonal

- How to recognize emotions
- Why emotions are important
- Avoiding the destructive expression of emotion and cultivating constructive ones

- Using emotions to distinguish between important and not so important projects
- Recognizing stress
- Developing coping strategies

Interpersonal

- Developing empathy
- Communication skills
- Engaging in safe relationships
- Dealing with conflict and bullying
- Negotiation and problem-solving skills
- Handling sex and intimacy

One recent study in the east of England measured emotional intelligence in 198 secondary school pupils using the Strengths and Difficulties Questionnaire and the Trait Emotional Intelligence Questionnaire (Whitehead, 2008). The findings were that children who scored high on the trait had better peer relationships, were less worrisome, possessed good coping strategies and were better behaved than those who scored low. Low-scoring pupils were also far more likely to be disruptive, to have been served with an exclusion notice or to have recorded unauthorized absences.

The study went on to show that a fairly small-scale educational project involving primary school children over two terms could improve classroom behaviour, peer relationships and coping strategies. The children were given activities that (a) helped them read facial expressions and other non-verbal cues, (b) role-played people in difficulty, (c) discussed possible responses to those difficulties, and (d) assisted them to keep a diary which logged their own and others' emotions and responses to a variety of triggers, such as the emotion of anger when being told to get on with work while also noting that the teacher himself might be worried about not getting things done.

Some possibilities

If we take Rousseau's prescriptions in *Emile* alongside the slow developing interest in emotional intelligence programmes in schools in Europe and the USA we can begin to see what a more complete programme in personal learning might look like alongside a traditional curriculum.

For ease of reference I will paragraph each item more or less in line with the summary of Rousseau's main points given earlier.

1. *A greater focus on personal learning in younger children.* One of Rousseau's enduring legacies is that younger children require a different kind of education from older children. Theorists and educators as diverse as John Dewey, Maria Montessori, Jean Piaget and Lev Vygotsky have followed him in this. Vygotsky in particular advocated

that early learning takes place when a gifted facilitator organizes the transmission of formal learning through cultural mediation:

> Every function in the child's cultural development appears twice: first, between people (interpsychological) and then inside the child (intrapsychological). This applies equally to voluntary attention, to logical memory, and to the formation of ideas. All the higher functions originate as actual relationships between individuals (Vygotsky, 1978: page 57).

The same applies to personal learning, if not more so, given that it offers training in both social intelligence and self-management.

2. *Self-esteem*. The child's estimation of her abilities arises twofold from her achievements but also, too, from her perception that she has the tools to handle social problems such as stress, bullying, academic pressure and personal handicaps. Self-esteem is also a function of the child's success in her relationships with other people. An early introduction to this success is therefore a prerequisite for that *amour-de-soi* which Rousseau saw as essential to a full commitment to self-development.

3. *Evading negative self-estimations*. This is not an issue that Rousseau seems to have addressed directly although a failure to acquire *amour-de-soi* would logically result in self-disparagement. That, in turn, would lead to such undesirable outcomes as reduced risk-taking, withdrawal from social intercourse, premature abandonment of study tasks and (possibly) increased involvement in disruptive behaviour. The solution is not to change the pupil's thinking about low self-esteem but to enlarge her access to problem-solving activities.

4. *Understanding emotion*. As I have already written elsewhere (Eaton, 2005), emotions are released by the organism in response to environmental cues in order to signal to the person that a particular class of action is required. For example, fear is a call for the person to seek help or experiment with safer modes of action; anger prompts us towards self-assertion; sadness drives us towards intimacy with others. Understanding emotion is a key for self-management when things get difficult. Without this understanding the pupil is likely to give up when it would be better to try a different approach. One 14-year old client of mine is a case in point. He would typically get frustrated when asked to write exercises in English composition (he is dyslexic and easily gets bogged down in grammatical difficulties). Once he learned that his frustration was not a sign of 'failure' but a call for him to take a break, work on some other aspect of the assignment or ask for assistance, he was able to add to his repertoire of coping strategies.

5. *Relationships*. Relationship management, along with emotional intelligence, is central to personal learning. Under this heading pupils learn the difference between unhealthy and healthy relationships. We might define this difference in Rousseau's terms: a healthy relationship is based on mutual *amour-de-soi*, in which compassion, understanding and

mutual give and take are all basic. However, the key skill here is empathy, which the child acquires typically through role-play and guided imagination.

6. *Communication*. For Rousseau, as for Vygotsky, good communicational habits are primarily learned through observation of parents, teachers and other models. On a personal learning programme the facilitator expands the child's emotional vocabulary ('Sounds like you're angry with X for not sharing his toys'); explains situations ('I'm upset because I can't find my bag'); provides tuition ('When we get scared that's usually a sign that we need help'); encourages empathy ('I wonder what Jessica felt when her friend said that?'); provides options ('Shouting when you're angry means people will just ignore you…you could come and talk to me about it first'); and praise and reinforcement.

7. *Self-management*. This final heading includes a number of loosely connected abilities: engaging with authority; reasoning for oneself; relating actions to consequences and negotiation skills. They all depend, crucially, on the application of formal reasoning outside the curriculum to the messier domains of emotions, personal agency and relationships.

Summary

For reasons of space this chapter has been, in the main, suggestive rather than discursive. My foremost purpose has been to keep the debate going on the importance of placing what is usually called 'emotional intelligence' in schools and pointing to the potential benefits of doing so. I hope also to have shown that what I have called personal learning might have some useful historical antecedents.

Notes

1   Rousseau's ideas are actually an extension of a critique of education by John Locke, first published in 1693, *Some Thoughts Concerning Education*. Both Locke and Rousseau concern themselves with the prior development of virtue and character in the child as a sound basis for intellectual learning.

2   Rousseau drew some distinctions between men and women that we would not apply today. His comments on Emile referred to male education and, in order to be consistent with Rousseau's text, I am using masculine pronouns here.

3   The twin terms 'intrapersonal' and 'interpersonal' intelligence are preferred to the more widely used label 'emotional intelligence' (Goleman, 1995) as they are both more precise and they also distinguish between personal and social intelligence. It is significant that many tests used to measure emotional intelligence – particularly those used in schools – actually focus on the inter-related skills of emotional self-management and relationship/communication.

15 The impact of modern communication technology on education

Wim Veen and Jan-Paul van Staalduinen

Introduction

Modern communication technologies shape the views of the new generation of students on the world around them (Tapscott, 1998; Collis and Moonen, 2001; Oblinger and Oblinger, 2005; Veen and Jacobs, 2005; Beck and Wade, 2006; Veen and Vrakking 2006). Due to their preference for television and internet technology, this generation has been called Homo Zappiens (Veen and Vrakking, 2006), or the Net Generation (Oblinger and Oblinger, 2005). Prominent characteristics of Homo Zappiens include their preference for images and symbols, their seemingly effortless adoption of technology and their cooperation and sharing in networks. They use technology in a functional manner, not touching what they cannot use and, increasingly, this generation seems to take exploration and learning, discovering the world, into their own hands. Homo Zappiens chooses its own frameworks for developing itself and structures the information that technology is making ever more pervasive.

Through the use of technology, Homo Zappiens learns to develop new skills and exhibits new behaviour that may show us a way of how education will be organized in the future. Homo Zappiens learns to participate in society through networks, switching between streams of information and learning to cooperate and share in getting relevant information. This chapter explores the impact of ICT on learners and the way in which students with the capacity for multi-tasking, combined with unprecedented access to knowledge, will change education.

Characteristics of new generation

Homo Zappiens is the generation that was born in the mid 90s of the twentieth century when the internet took off, becoming a commodity in many households of western

Europe. Technology has noticeably influenced the characteristics and competences of Homo Zappiens, which are described in Table 15.1.

Table 15.1 Characteristics of the Homo Zappiens

Characteristic	Description
Iconic preferences	Homo Zappiens' preference for icons is a very necessary attitude to survive in an era where older generations are confronted with 'information overload', yet Homo Zappiens seems capable of handling this phenomenon (Veen and Vrakking, 2006). In its communications with peers Homo Zappiens uses icons and abbreviations as well. Lindström and Seybold (2003) have labelled this language of shortcuts 'TweenSpeak'.
Technology is air	Homo Zappiens is merely interested in technology if it works and will just as easily pick up something else if that suits their needs better. They often have little understanding of the fundamentals of the technology they are using, yet they can explain the functions that make a tool useful. Tapscott (1998) formulates this perception of technology as: 'It doesn't exist. It's like the air'.
Inversed education	Up to about the age of five, children seem to ask their parents how to use a personal computer. From the age of six most children have learned how to use the personal computer and will often resort first to asking friends before asking their parents. From the age of eight upwards, this generation is educating their parents on how to use PCs (Veen and Jacobs, 2005). This 'inverse education' is typical for this generation.
Networking is their lifestyle	To the Net Generation, living in networks is as normal as breathing. Homo Zappiens' networks include both virtual and physical networks. They are almost constantly connected to electronic networks, through which they stay in contact with their friends and a wide source of information available.
Cooperation	Homo Zappiens has made the use of networks as a lifestyle. They use their network of contacts to provide them with the information they need and if this network does not suffice, they ask an online community consisting of many individuals they do not know, but who are willing to help. For the Homo Zappiens, knowledge sharing is common even with those they do not know at all.
Virtual is real	Youth today does not make the same distinction between the 'real' world and the 'virtual' world that so much of society still does. To them, when they communicate with a friend through chat or in a game, this communication is no less real than a physical meeting. Communities and social networks appear to be physical, virtual and hybrid at the same time. (Oblinger and Oblinger, 2005).
Multiple identities	Homo Zappiens has online and face to face identities as is illustrated by a boy describing a friend: 'Online he is okay, but at school he is a nerd'. (Veen and Jacobs, 2005). Young people are accustomed to playing with different characters or roles and feel the consequences of these different roles as other gamers react to them.

Characteristic	Description
Multitasking	These children seem to be online, watch TV, talk on the phone, listen to the radio and write a document, apparently all at the same time. (Oblinger and Oblinger, 2005). Children seem to divide their attention across the different information flows, focusing only on one, but keeping a lower level of attention on the others. By using their attention flexibly, Homo Zappiens seems capable of handling much more information than previous generations (Veen and Vrakking, 2006).
Critical evaluation	As a consequence of multitasking, they instantly and almost subconsciously value different streams of information to decide where to place their attention. Homo Zappiens is confronted with a lot of information, not all of it to be taken at face value. Critical evaluation is what children do when selecting and filtering information flows.
Zapping	Homo Zappiens seems to show a zapping behaviour that is specifically aiming at filtering information from different programmes at a time. The purpose is to get the message in order to understand (Veen and Vrakking, 2006). It allows them to select only those bits of information from each channel that are critical for understanding what the programme is all about.
Instant pay-off	The Net Generation has little patience and short attention spans. Their skills are aimed at processing various flows of different information quickly, but they have also come to expect this kind of high density information streaming; anything less and they will become bored. Lindström and Seybold (2003) label them the 'Instant Generation'.
Self-confidence through self-direction	ICT offers youth control over not just devices, but communication, networks and situations as well; situations which they will often have to master as adults (Tapscott, 1998). Through the use of technology, this generation has added options for exploring their own individualism. Games are a prime example of this, as they allow any gamer an infinite number of tries to attempt to reach certain goals.

The impact of technology on learning

Technology has taken dominance over society as a means of providing organization to our lives. Immersion, interactivity and communication are critical characteristics of the technologies Homo Zappiens has been using from early childhood on. This has important implications for learning and educational organizations. The impact of this can be seen in the behaviour of Homo Zappiens:

- In a world where technology is available, the most important skills are those that enable us to use that technology to enrich our lives (Laurillard 1993; Harper, Rodden, Rogers and Sellen, 2008). That is why Homo Zappiens adopts the use new technology at an amazing pace. At the same time they seem to be paying less attention to learning mathematical skills, grammar and memorization; rather, they rely on calculators and search engines to provide them with the same information. The cause of this is not so much a disinterest in 'old concepts', but much more often a form of prioritizing skills.

- On the internet, communities of people gather information that is relevant to them and recommend it to others within the community (Wenger, 1998). Through a form of internal recommendation, information is filtered based on perceived value and importance. Cooperation thus provides a mechanism for distributing the increasingly larger task of determining which information is valuable.
- People used to keep their most prized knowledge and competences private, and thus scarce, but nowadays we now let others know about our knowledge and skills. In an organizational system that promoted competition, keeping knowledge private made sense. Yet in a network where negotiation and communication are the most important elements (Steeples and Jones 2002), the need for privacy is an outdated concept, and the need for attention becomes key.

Given the rise of interactive network technology, the logical direction for education and learning to develop as society ever more embraces the uniqueness of each individual, is for the process of learning to become more natural. As people can learn from any new experience and what they learn often is unpredictable, there isn't a real way in which the optimum level of development for each individual can be reached through structured education. Accepting that the outcome of learning cannot be controlled upfront would lead to a more natural form of learning. Setting goals for education is contradictory to natural learning. A better approach would be to use increasing levels of difficulty for each student as they demonstrate increased abilities, leaving each to explore their skills at their own level (Christensen, Horn and Johnson, 2008). Technological advances have made it possible for people to start learning this non-linear way; our most natural way of learning (Siemens, 2006).

Four changing forces

Education will evolve due to these new student generations demanding different pedagogical approaches and technological environments. Future students will not follow courses by reading an online book or watching some streaming videos, but will enrol for projects within a knowledge community. Those projects revolve around solving a specific problem through discussion or writing a scientific paper, every project having an end product (Collis and Moonen, 2001)! In the future, learning will be about externalizing the knowledge of participants. The major goal of learning will be to co-create new knowledge. And the role of teachers will be to structure discussions and monitor the quality of work being done (Collis and Moonen, 2001). Within this collaborative system, individual students can be assessed in terms of competences and experience, as presented through their (online) portfolios. As all students have individual, and thus unique, learning histories (Diepstraten, 2006), this will impact the value of qualifications granted by individual institutions, obsolescing them eventually.

Three other developments will force education to adapt to new demands. First, in addition to initial education, learning will become a work-based activity for many employees. From this group there will be less demand for traditional courses either; employees will be instead be keen to participate in online communities focusing on their work-related needs. Education will function as validation centres for them, rather than training centres.

Secondly, technology will continue to evolve and mixed realities and virtual realities will further enhance our opportunities to reduce scarcity of presence. We will be able to meet, work together and discuss using spectacles and facilities such as caves where we can shape our ideas and design products or models. Higher education will become technology centres where ever developing technologies will enable customers to take advanced learning experiences.

Finally, restricting borders between the mono-disciplines will be overcome by increasing multi-disciplinary challenges with sustainability as a main goal. Increasing multi-disciplinarity in subject matter will force faculties in higher education and other educational institutions to restructure and reorganize. Faculties as buildings and boundaries to hold the mono-disciplines are to be reformed into college knowledge groups with the special ability to do particular multi-disciplinary challenges.

Future education will evolve towards service-oriented organizations for a wide variety of clients including initial, informal, post-academic and life-long learning trajectories. At university level, as far as their research activities are concerned, they will function as hubs in worldwide networks of excellence in both specialized and multi-disciplinary fields of study collaborating with industries aiming at validating their knowledge for society. They will become more like 'learning malls' for students and 'virtual research studios' for the research community, accessible from anywhere, appreciated among students according to scientific reputation. Van der Zanden (2009) describes this learning mall as a distributed electronic virtual knowledge centre equipped with personalized learning delivery agents. Every student, undergraduate, graduate, post-graduate, and other expert or professional has access to these future rings of universities where 'just in time', 'just enough' and 'just for you' learning objects are key. He argues that this learning mall is a logical outcome of four waves of technology impact (see Figure 15.1), enabling the ever changing demands of individual learners and society at large.

Figure 15.1 Stages of educational technologies versus ICT uses (Van der Zanden, 2004), based on (Nolan, 2000)

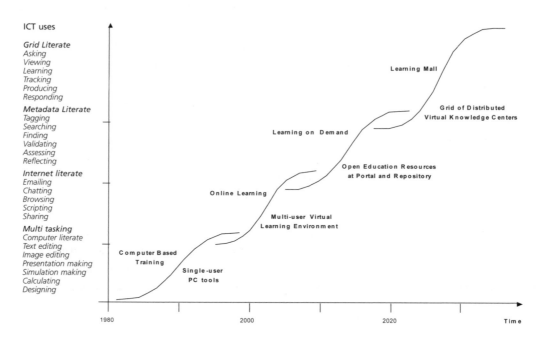

In learning malls students will enrol and work within virtual communities and go elsewhere, thus building their expertise, in many cases in close collaboration with industry. Higher education will become a sprawling, fluid learning network of universities, as illustrated in Figure 15.2, in which people are a part of constantly changing communities, attending and leaving different universities, for individual learning experiences.

Figure 15.2 Illustration of a learning network

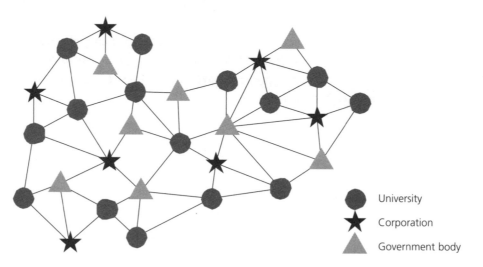

As a consequence, higher education institutions slowly evolve towards institutions that will function as hubs in knowledge networks, serving students working in fluid communities of research or learning on subjects of their interest. Life-long learning will become an integral part of the working life of individuals as networks will continue to exist between industry and higher education. This view might sound like a scenario unlikely to come true to its full extension. But looking at the way working teams are nowadays more often organized in an ad hoc manner or how coalitions shift allegiance with the shifting of political tides, we can already see how society has been increasingly incorporating the concept of flexible structures to the organization of dynamic reality. There are strong developments such as globalization, virtual communities sharing knowledge, and specialization among scientific institutions at a global level, indicating structures that will make any university that will not participate in this worldwide progress an isolated regional or local school. These developments of globalization and sharing knowledge at a global level will enhance the chances that institutions will adopt technology to enable their global orientation and, hence, create a higher education system that will suit future generations of learners.

Concluding comments

Realizing that essentially every experience in our lives may be a source of learning, we can choose three of the most important aspects for redesigning our educational settings. Most importantly, we should depart from the setting of goals upfront, because essentially these limit the experimentation that ultimately leads to increased competences. We should stimulate exaggerative, playful learning, realizing that all learning is essentially a continued refinement of more basic skills and understanding. We must also, rather than seeing learning as a means towards an end, encourage learning as a continuous process, stimulating increases in skill and competence with a decrease in structure and an increase in complexity, tailored to each individual's level of mastery.

Homo Zappiens is a major driving force behind these changes. Does this mean that all students nowadays are instantly capable of grasping these changes? Probably not; at first only the brightest ones will both affect and embrace these changes. Yet the rest will slowly, but surely, follow, their need for accommodation and pampering by their educational institutions fading.

Interleaf:
How I see the future

Steve Coates, age 20

People have always been intrigued by what the future will look like. In order to understand the future, we surely must first look at how we got to where we are. The world has changed greatly in the last 150 years, however humans are still driven by the same basic needs as they have been since they were formed: food, sleep, sex, the feeling of being appreciated or loved. Is this set to change in the foreseeable future? No.

Many believe that, with the advent of the increased use of technology, people will become socially detached, choosing instead to live a life in front of the computer screen. However the primal basic instincts of people will still need to be fulfilled; this will heavily influence technology's forward path.

There is a view that technology will enable people to revert to communities or villages where they no longer have to travel to work. The internet, perhaps the most significant invention of the twenty-first century, could enable a new form of 'workplace' in which people remain in their communities and can communicate and work with people across the world.

Perhaps schools and educational establishments as we know them will become vastly different to what we know as the 'norm'. Is it still necessary to have school buildings when children could, even now, log onto a website and virtually interact with the teacher and learn without restraint or time limits? Examples of this can already be seen with podcasting, video podcasting and live streaming, all readily available for free and available to all.

Music has changed hugely of recent years. It has been greatly affected by the internet and this in turn has led to a huge amount of 'illegal file sharing'. Many argue this has greatly damaged the music business, though perhaps this could be the best thing for music. Myspace is just one example of the internet being used by artists writing music in their bedrooms, to bypass the record companies which have for so long dominated what gets through to the public, and instead getting their creations 'out there' to their audiences.

It is possible, however, that there will be a struggle to get away from the constraints of technology. Will people go back to the way of living before technology? Can we return to life before technology? Perhaps one of the earliest examples of this theory in action are the Amish; small Christian religious denominations that form a very traditional sub-grouping of Mennonite churches. The Amish have taken a stance of resistance to the adoption of many modern technologies. While this may initially seem over the top, will the people of the future want to remove themselves from the technological world to retain the communities in which they've thrived?

Social networking sites such as Facebook, Myspace and Bebo have enabled individuals to communicate on a very global level, easily interacting with people in different towns and even on different continents. Communities will be profoundly affected by the capabilities that the internet is bringing to individual communications, granting individuals in a once isolating city the ability to easily establish relationships with others in their area by first meeting online. From hobby clubs to political organizations to social networking, the internet will change expectations of geographically oriented community organizations, and provide increasingly wide choices to individuals who wish to participate in local communities that share their interests. Not everything about the internet is global; an interconnected world is also locally interconnected. The internet will increasingly be used for communications within communities as much as across countries.

I am currently studying a BA (Hons) degree course in Interactive Media Production. This course focuses heavily on the skills required to develop what many predict the internet will no doubt become. This ranges from graphic and web design, software programming and many other skills so to enable the increment of the interactive tools of the future. I cannot see myself ever working in what we have called an 'office', instead I see my 'workspace ' as being anywhere with a computer. A virtual office space that I can carry with me wherever I go. The future requires not simply learning skills, but also continuing to develop and formulate innovative ways to get the most of the new resources continually being created as technology develops. My future is not about a lifetime of employment but a lifetime of employability.

16 Deckchairs on the *Titanic*

Max Coates

The contributors to this book could be divided into two groups: 'pragmatists' and 'prophets'. The former would argue that the UK's educational system needs some degree of reformation. The 'prophets', on the other hand, gesture towards a speculative future, which is often ill-defined, and argue for root and branch transformation.

Imagine that you are invited to join John West-Burnham, Paul Clarke and Russell Rook for dinner. John urbane, Paul good company but perhaps a little more rustic in style. Russ, the streetwise academic and ethicist. Inevitably the conversation turns to education. You realize that you are in for a rollercoaster ride without a moderating pragmatist in sight.

Each of the three interjects with a different perspective. John engages with the limiting contribution of the school improvement model. He argues that educational systems are often forged from the tension between:

- *Equity* which is about securing access to education that is not impeded by poverty, social class, gender, race or learning disability.
- *Efficiency*, in essence, getting the best pupil outcomes for the substantial expenditure made on education.
- *Excellence*, the judgement call about the outputs of the educational system, though of course the nature of this is the subject of much debate.

Putting his glass down, he points out that frequently one dimension can dominate to the detriment of the others. Getting into his stride he reflects that:

> Schooling as a social process emerged in the late nineteenth and early twentieth centuries in a culture of deference, dependence and compliance. The vast majority of the population was prepared for lives in factories, on farms, as servants and to be slaughtered in their thousands at the whim of incompetent generals. This was all possible in a society that believed in a natural hierarchy of ability and saw an individual's potential being fixed and determined at birth (West-Burnham, 2005: page 19).

Rooted in philosophy and historical precedent, he concludes that:

> Reconciling equity, efficiency and excellence has to be the goal of every policy maker in a democracy.

He further argues that:

> There is a wealth of evidence to suggest that in many education systems, attempts to do so at both a macro and a micro level are failing. As the cost of education continues to rise, there is not a commensurate increase in measurable performance. The socially disadvantaged continue to be systematically marginalized by the structure of school systems. As standards rise, so the debate about excellence is refined to reinforce elitist models of achievement (2005: page 12).

The hiatus surrounding the arrival of the main course creates a space for Paul to take up the discourse. Apocalyptic in style, he outlines the inevitable consequences of a high consumption economy. A realist rather than a default pessimist, he confronts the spectre of an oil-depleted world and global migration resulting from the desertification of countries by modest temperature increase.

Paul's argument is deceptively simple, highlighting the conflict and contrast between an education system predicated on consumerism and a future lived in the reality of exhausted resources. Gesturing and with frustration in his voice, he pleads for education to take up the sustainability agenda with an accelerating passion. With a slight, almost imperceptible, shake of his head he cites examples of sustainable curriculum development: a school-based fish farm supplying local restaurants, allotments on school sites, community involvement in schools and even challenging the Enclosure Act. The food obviously sparks a train of thought as he explains how coriander is growing well on the hillsides once populated by sheep in Lancashire. The story unfolds of a post-industrial community progressively reformatting.

Russ takes up the theme, as he expresses his deep commitment to the regeneration of communities. He charts the shift in his own thinking from imposed re-engineering to indigenous empowerment. He advances a parallel with the health service as a move from a medical model with interventions such as vaccination towards personally driven, responsible lifestyle choices. There is a case made for diverse bottom up revolution, which is rooted in local communities, as opposed to imposed systemic change. Warming to his theme, the warp of structural change becomes shot through with the weft of values, hope, community and the evolution of compassionate humanity.

This is powerful discourse fuelled with prophetic passion. Diners on nearby tables have fallen silent and are eavesdropping on the dialogue, drawn by the advocacy of hope and transformation. The meal concludes, the settling of the tab reflecting the strident altruism of the three. As they leave there is a strong feeling that they have reinforced each other's thinking and increased their personal resolve to ferment educational revolution.

The fictional diners, like many of the other contributors to this book, have the luxury and mandate to envision and explore change. They are passionate prophets.

The majority of people involved in education might look wistfully at such unfettered thinking while others would dismiss such speculation as irritating and detached from the real world, though I am often left with a feeling that the latter might be the more Pratchettesque creation.

The book offers repeated challenges to our extant education system and to generate more relevant alternatives. Consider the following two pieces of work. Firstly the research undertaken by Broadfoot, Claxton and Deakin-Crick (2005), exploring how individuals learn and suggesting that this is very different to the experience of many in their school context. Their work has brought this into sharp focus with their development at the University of Bristol's Effective Lifelong Learning Inventory (ELLI). This work identified seven key dimensions that supported an individual's motivation or power to learn. These included developing resilience as a learner, the ability to make meaning, critical curiosity, creativity and learning relationships. The research concluded that over time, and particularly through the course of formal learning, children currently become weaker as sustained learners. At the same time they become more dependent on teachers and others to help them learn and less able to cope with mistakes and failure.

The second piece of research comes from the Mckinsey/Barber Education Report (2007). Two 'exhibits' are highlighted here. In the United States of America public spending on education has risen between 1980 and 2005 by 73 per cent per student. This calculation allowed for inflation. It was noted that over the same period more teachers were employed, the student: teacher ratio fell by 18 per cent and that by 2005 class sizes were the smallest that they had even been. Thousands of initiatives had been launched, all aimed at improving the quality of education in their national schools.

During the measured period student outcomes, as measured by their own Department of Education's national assessment program, stayed almost the same. The report noted (page 13) that there was some improvement in mathematics, however the reading scores of 9 year olds, 13 year olds and 17 year olds remained the same in 2005 as they had in 1980.

The second, and perhaps more striking, findings cited in the report came from research from the Organisation for Economic and Co-operative Development. Almost every country in the OECD made substantial increases in expenditure in education through a similar period. There was a general trend to launch multiple initiatives to drive the 'value for money' agenda. Despite this, very few systems actually delivered an improvement; most flatlined or showed deterioration. The report cites Pritchett (2003) as follows (page 15):

Table 16.1 Spending and outcomes in the OECD

Country	Increase in real expenditure per student (1970–1994)	Increase in student achievement (1970–1994)
Belgium	65%	–5%
United Kingdom	77%	–8%
Japan	103%	2%
Germany	108%	–5%
Italy	126%	1%
France	212%	–7%
New Zealand	223%	–10%
Australia	270%	–2%

At the worst these statistics are devastating, at the best they are at least challenging.

The *Titanic* sank in April 1912 and the tragedy has continued to fuel stories and speculation. Among other items it was carrying were 1500 fruit knives, 1250 lbs of jam, 2500 lbs of sausages and a deep conviction that the vessel was invincible. After the ship hit an iceberg the Vice President of the Star Line, Phillip Franklin, commented to reporters

> There is no danger that *Titanic* will sink. The boat is unsinkable and nothing but inconvenience will be suffered by the passengers.

There were many stories that came out the sinking; some heroic and some shameful. Perhaps even stranger were the accounts of people playing cards and dancing as the ship was sinking. Ultimately this spawned the phrase 'moving deckchairs on the *Titanic*', a phrase often used to describe behaviours detached from the reality of an impending and urgent situation. Many contributors to this book are claiming just that. In essence our education system is ultimately not equipping young people to face the challenges of our emerging context. Essential to a reformulated education must be cohesive values, sustainability, creativity, team-working skills and resilience. There is still an excessive emphasis on a content-driven curriculum in an age where the teacher is no longer the gatekeeper of knowledge and where content is ephemeral and constantly superseded. Alvin Toffler wrote an apposite summary and critique of such a content-focused approach:

> The illiterate of the 21st Century will not be those who cannot read and write but those who cannot learn, unlearn and relearn. (1970: page 323)

Education is an enterprise of huge significance in whatever way it is viewed. Its development is driven by many factors, which are seldom held as a set by the players.

The following is almost certainly not an exhaustive list of such factors but may well shed some light on the uncertain path education seems to walk.

Policy Most educational systems are perceived as requiring national delivery. They are usually prescribed by the key budget holder. The problem is that it is not unusual for government policy to lag behind contemporary events by perhaps two generations. Education has become a leviathan which must be corralled at all costs. In turn this process tends to engender a managerial mindset. Extensive policy always requires extensive bureaucracy and often a heavy burden of accountability.

Practice This is not about serving a pedagogical apprenticeship but rather the development of practice through evidence and research. Regrettably much that enters education is highly speculative and born out of assumption rather than rigour. This is especially the case with reference to learning theory and is well illustrated by such initiatives as the rather eccentric 'Brain Gym'.

Pragmatism This is a consequence of both personality and pressure. Many individuals are predisposed to the practical and can even make it sound a virtue: 'We are here to teach not experiment'. I was even told by one comprehensive school deputy head that 'this learning stuff is OK, but it doesn't get kids through exams and meet targets'. There was also the head of boys' grammar school who wanted to know why a conference was on learning: 'Wasn't that the job of the primary schools and secondary schools, after all, are here to tell pupils what they need to know'. Both these accounts are drawn from the last three years. Excessive commitment to pragmatism tends to generate replication rather than evolution. Further, an education system where initiatives and workload are unbridled creates pressure and a culture which is susceptible to quick fixes. Reflective practice and deadlines do not form an easy partnership.

Prejudice We have made great strides in tackling prejudice as it relates to ethnicity, gender and disability. It is arguable that less progress has been made in the area of professional understanding. By way of an example, consider IQ. This is a dubious concept, which assumes that genetics (with a bit of nurture) has allocated each individual with a 'core processor'. The fortunate have an 'Intel Dual Core' while the less blessed are deemed to be running on something rescued from an Amstrad. There is also a common belief that IQ and postcode might be in someway linked. Understanding has moved on; it is widely held that intelligence has a significant degree of plasticity and can be developed and that a more useful model is that of multiple intelligences. There are many other areas where prejudice exerts an excessive influence and supplants true professionalism.

Polemic The voice of dissent or protest. Such contrary discourses are framed with varying degrees of skill and conviction. There is always a danger that a movement of protest may lean to heavily on rhetoric rather than rationality. Many of the speeches at education conferences fall into this category.

Philosophy In my initial teacher education I was confronted with the ideas of Plato, Dewey, Rousseau and then sent on a teaching practice in Stratford in the east end of

London. At the time I was nonplussed. Now it makes huge sense as significant perspectives were provided from which education can be reformulated. However, such a grounding is missing for many new entrants. Education is not simply informed by research but also by big picture-thinking around ethics and values. Citizenship is not just about voting habits but about the conceptualization of society and the rights and responsibility of those who comprise it. Consider discipline; a Taser will contain classroom behaviour but will it contribute towards the formation of participants in a civil society? Currently, I would suggest that this is the weakest area of educational thinking.

Passion Ideas without drive or motivation will soon seem fabrications without force. Every movement from the Ragged Schools, Montessori Schools and even to the comprehensive schools was birthed in passion. Of course, the danger is that as the ideas are scaled up they become fainter like a photocopy of a photocopy of a photocopy.

There is a need for all of the above except prejudice. I would argue that creating a new educational landscape will benefit from the principles derived from a clear philosophy fuelled by passion. The complexity of our current context allied to the uncertainties of the future would seem to favour imaginative trial projects or pilots. These must be designed so that advantages may accrue but that they do no harm.

There is a need to explore change from the bottom up and then capture the learning from such enterprises and disseminate this. A system with over 24,000 schools is not likely to be responsive to instantaneous systemic change. Permission has to granted to experiment and innovate. Obviously this was the mandate of The Innovation Unit. However, it was surprising how few schools took advantage of the opportunity to seek disapplication. Perhaps the message is to search out and nurture innovation rather than try to mutate 'what is' through imposed processes.

One of the most striking ground-up developments has to be the early years provision in Reggio a Emilia in Italy. Attempts to define good quality childcare usually rely on quantifiable indicators such as staff/child ratios. However, experience from other countries suggests that we might do better to reflect on the totality of a child's experience, and that the best early years services are based on a child-centred understanding of education. Young children's services in this Italian city, and the pedagogical theory on which they are based, have a worldwide reputation. Lisa Harker writing in the *Guardian* (2004) concluded:

> Their approach is informed by an image of the child, not as an empty vessel into which the right ingredients must be poured, but as a being with extraordinary potential. Great emphasis is placed on encouraging curiosity and innovation, with both children and teachers engaged in a constant process of discovery. The child is not seen as a passive recipient of education or care, but as an active participant. Staff are confident and articulate, and parents are encouraged to be involved. The outcomes are neither predeterminable nor necessarily measurable. But countless testimonies suggest they offer children the strongest foundation for life.

Perhaps it is at the level of the community facilitated by committed visionaries who have a compelling vision of the future that new landscapes are indeed formed and created. Ecosystems survive challenge and threat by the presence of biodiversity. Monocultures are vulnerable to change. Arguably the same Darwinian perspective can be applied to education. A monolithic system could be apposite but it could also be inappropriate and indeed fail to equip its citizens for a transitional future. There is a case for the promotion of edudiversity but then that is a bold step to take. Entrepreneurs are unlikely to be developed and nurtured in a climate of compliance and conformity.

Afterword: Juba Diocesan Model Secondary School

Juba is the capital of Southern Sudan, situated on the River Nile, and with a population of c.500,000. From 1983–2005, because of civil war, the town was cut off from the outside world and under the rule of a military governor. There are 11 church primary schools in the town, half established by refugees for their young children under very basic conditions. There was, however, a lack of secondary education. The Sudanese Church has a link with Salisbury Diocese and, with the signing of the Comprehensive Peace Agreement in 2005, a plea was made for help.

The response resulted in the building of a secondary school which was opened on 1 May 2007. The school is designed for 360 students in nine classrooms covering three school years (equivalent to Years 9, 10 and 11 in the British system.) It is a fee-paying school (GBP150 per year) and, to enable orphans and children from low-income families to attend, a support group in Salisbury has found sponsors to provide individual bursaries of GBP100. An example is 22-year-old Viktor who is an orphan and recently returned from Kenya where he was in the army. He was working in Juba as a night watchman in order to pay his fees but he now has a bursary.

The school is currently suffering growing pains. Development plans for the schools establishment mean that considerable, ongoing financial assistance will be necessary to sustain the initiative.

www.salisburyanglican.org.uk

Bibliography

Adams S. (1996), *The Dilbert Principle*. New York: Harper Collins.

ATL, DfES, GMB, NAHT, NASUWT, NEOST, PAT, SHA, TGWU, UNISON, WAG (2003), *Raising Standards and Tackling Workload: A National Agreement*. London: DfES.

Adonis, A. (2007), Speech at the HMC Annual Conference.

Baker, M. http://news.bbc.co.uk/1/hi/education. Accessed 23 May 2009.

Barber, M. and Mourshed, M. (2007), *McKinsey Education Report*. London.

Beck, J. C., and Wade, M. (2006), *The Kids are Alright: How the Gamer Generation is Changing the Workplace*. Boston: Harvard Business School Press.

Bentley, T. (2005), *Future's Thinking*. Nottingham NCSL video.

Best, B. (2008), *We Did it Here!* Carmarthen: Crown House Publishing.

Birol, F. (2008), *World Energy Outlook*. Paris: International Energy Agency.

Bottery, M. (2004), *The Challenges of Educational Leadership: Values in a Globalized Age*. London: Paul Chapman.

Bottery, M. (2007), 'Reports from the Front Line: English Headteachers' Work in an Era of Practice Centralisation', *Educational Management Administration and Leadership*, Vol. 35, No. 1, 89–110.

Boudrillard, J. (1988), *Simulcra and Simulation*, (trans. Glaser, S.) Michigan: University of Michigan.

Broadfoot, P., Claxton, G., Deakin-Crick, R. (2005), *The Effective Lifelong Learning Inventory*, www.bristol.ac.uk/education/enterprise/elli. Accessed 27 May 2009.

Brown, L. (2002,) *Eco-economy: Building an Economy for the Earth*. Washington: Earth Policy Institute.

Burbules, C. and Torres, C. (2000), *Globalisation and Education: Critical Perspectives*. New York: Routledge.

Caldwell, B. (2006), *Re-imagining Educational Leadership*. London: ACER Press and Sage.

Chapman, G., Ainscow, M., Bragg, J., Gunter, H., Hull, J., Mongon, D., Muijs, D., and West, M. (2007), *Emerging Patterns of School Leadership: Current Practice and Future Directions*. Nottingham: NCSL.

Christensen, C. M., Horn, M. B., and Johnson, C. W. (2008), *Disrupting Class: How Disruptive Innovation will Change the Way the World Learns*. New York: McGraw-Hill.

Clarke, P. (2008), 'Education and Sustainability', *Professional Development Today*. vol. 11, no. 1.

Clarke, P. (2009), 'Sustainability and Improvement: a Problem of and for Education', *Improving Schools*. vol. 12, no. 1, 11–17.

Cohen. G. A., (2000), *Karl Marx's Theory of History: A Defence*. Oxford: Oxford University Press.

Collarbone, P. (2009), *Creating Tomorrow: Planning, Developing and Sustaining Change in Education and Other Public Services*. London: Network Continuum.

Collarbone, P. and West-Burnham, J. (2008), *Understanding Systems Leadership: Securing Excellence and Equity in Education*. London: Network Continuum.

Collis, B., and Moonen, J. (2001), *Flexible Learning in a Digital World*. London: Kogan Page Limited.

Cowie, E. and Cowie, L. (2004), *That One Idea: Nathaniel Woodard and His Schools*. Abbots Bromley: Woodard Foundation.

Curren, R. (ed.) (2006), *Philosophy of Education: an Anthology*. London: Blackwell.

Davies, B. and Ellison, L. (1990) *Strategic Direction and Development of the School*. London: Routledge.

DCSF (2007), *The Children's Plan: Building Brighter Futures*. London: The Stationery Office.

DCSF (2008a), *Building Brighter Futures: Next Steps for the Children's Workforce*. Nottingham: DCSF Publications.

DCSF (2008b), *School Teachers' Pay and Conditions Document*. London: The Stationery Office.

DCSF (2008c), *21st Century Schools: A World-Class Education for Every Child*. Nottingham: DCSF Publications.

DCSF (2008d), *2020 Children and Young People's Workforce Strategy*. Nottingham: DCSF Publications.

de Botton, A. (2005), *Status Anxiety*. London: Penguin.

de Botton, A. (2009), *The Pleasures and Sorrows of Work*. London: Hamish Hamilton.

Deiniger and Squire World Bank Inequality Database (2008) in *International Encyclopedia of the Social Sciences*. Farmington Hills: Thomson Gale.

DfES (1998), *Teachers: Meeting the Challenge of Change*. London: The Stationery Office.

DfES (2001), *Schools Achieving Success*. White Paper on Secondary Schools. Annesley: The Stationery Office.

DfES (2002), *Time for Standards: Reforming the School Workforce*. Nottingham: DfES Publications.

DfES (2004), *National Standards for Headteachers*. Nottingham: DfES Publications.

Diepstraten, I. (2006), *De Nieuwe Leerder: Trendsettende Leerbiografieën in Een Kennissamenleving*. Tilburg: F&N Boekservice.

Eaton, J. & Johnson, R. (2001), *Communicate with Emotional Intelligence*. Oxford: How To Books.

Eaton, J. (2005), *Reverse Therapy for Health*. www.reverse therapy.com/Resources_&_Self_Help.

Edwards, C.M., *Future's Thinking (and How to Do It)*. London: Demos. Accessed 2 May 2009.

Finger, M. And Asún, J. M. (2001), *Adult Education at the Crossroads: Learning our Way Out*. London: Zed Books.

Fromm E. (1997), *To Have or to Be*. London: Continuum.

Fukuyama. F. (1993), *The End of History and the Last Man*. London: Penguin.

Fullan, M. (1998), 'Leadership for the 21st Century: Breaking the Bonds of Dependency', *Educational Leadership*. vol. April 1998 55 7.

Fullan, M. (2001), *Leading in a Culture of Change*. San Francisco: Jossey-Bass.

Gajardo, M, (1994) 'Ivan Illich' in Z. Morsy (ed.) *Key Thinkers in Education*. vol.2. Paris: UNESCO Publishing.

Gardner, H. (1993), *Frames of Mind*. London: Fontana.

Gardner, H. (1999), *The Disciplined Mind*. New York: Simon and Schuster.

Goldspink, C. (2007). 'Rethinging Educational Reform: a Loosely Coupled and Complex Systems Perspective', *Educational Management Administration & Leadership*. vol. 35, no. 1, 27–50.

Goleman, D. (1996), *Emotional Intelligence*. London: Bloomsbury.

Goleman, D. (1998), *Working with Emotional Intelligence*. London: Bloomsbury.

Greenfield, S. (2000), *Brain Story*. London: BBC Worldwide Limited.

Guardian (16 April 2009), 'Nuclear plans "too slow to stop lights going out"' .

Hallinger, P. (2009), *Assessing the Contribution of Distributed Leadership to School Improvement and Growth in Math Achievement*, AERA Conference Paper, San Diego, April 2009.

Halstead M. and Taylor M. J. (1995), *Values in Education and Education in Values.* Abingdon: Routledge.

Handy, C. (1993), *Understanding Organizations,* 4th ed. Oxford: Oxford University Press.

Hargreaves, D. (1994), *The Mosaic of Learning: Schools and Teachers for the New Century.* London: Demos.

Harker, L. (2004), 'Lessons from Reggio Emilia', The *Guardian*, 11 November 2004.

Harper, R., Rodden, T., Rogers, Y., and Sellen, A. (eds.) (2008), *Being Human: Human-Computer Interaction in the year 2020.* Cambridge: Microsoft Research Ltd.

Harris, A. (2008), *Distributed School Leadership: Developing Tomorrow's Leaders*. London: Routledge Falmer Press.

Harvey-Jones, J. (1994), *All Together Now*. London: Heinemann.

Hauerwas, S. (1981), *A Community of Character.* Chicago: Notre Dame.

Hauerwas, S. (2001), 'Virtues in Public', *Christian Existence Today.* Grand Rapids: Brazos Press.

Heeney, B (1969), *Mission to the Middle Classes – The Woodard Schools 1848–1891*. Abbots Bromley: The Woodard Foundation.

Heifetz, R. (1994), *Leadership Without Easy Answers.* Cambridge: Belknap Press.

Hern, M. (ed.) (1996), *Deschooling Our Lives.* Gabriola Island: New Society Publishers.

HM Government (2002), The Education Act 2002. London: Her Majesty's Stationery Office.

HM Government (2004), The Children Act 2004. London: Her Majesty's Stationery Office.

HM Treasury (2003), Every Child Matters. Norwich: The Stationery Office.

Hobsbawm, E. (2009), 'Socialism has failed. Now capitalism is bankrupt. So what comes next?'. The *Guardian*. 10 April 2009.

Hock, D. (1999), *Birth of the Chaordic Age*. San Francisco: Barrett and Koehler.

Holmes, B. (1965), *Problems in Education*, London: Routledge and Kegan Paul.

Holmes, B. (1981), *Comparative Education: Some Considerations of Method.* London: Allen and Unwin.

Hopkins, D., Highham, R. and Antaridou, E. (2009), *School Leadership in England: Contemporary Challenges, Innovative Responses and Future Trends.* Nottingham: NCSL.

Howard-Jones, P. (2006), *Neuroscience and Education.* London: TLRP.

Huizinga, J. (1938), *Homo Ludens*. Haarlem: Tjeenk Willink.

Hutchins, E. T. (1995), *Cognition in the Wild.* Cambridge: MIT.

Hutton, W. (2007), *The Writing on the Wall: China and the West in the 21st Century.* London: Little, Brown.

James, C., Connolly, M., Dunning, G. and Elliott, T. (2007). 'Systemic Leadership for Schools and the Significance of Systemic Authorisation', *Educational Management Administration & Leadership,* vol. 35, no. 4, 573–588.

James, O. (2007), *Affluenza*. London: Random House.

Illich, I. (1975), *Medical Nemesis: The Expropriation of Health*. London: Marian Boyars.

Illich, I. and Verne, E. (1976,) *Imprisoned in the Global Classroom*. London: Writers and Readers Publishing Co-operative.

Jaeger, W. (1945), *Paideia*. (trans. G. Highet). Oxford: Oxford University Press.

Joyce, B. and Showers, B. (1988), *Student Achievement Through Staff Development*. White Plains: Longman.

Kelly, A. (2009), 'Education Futures and Schooling Theory: Adapting Sen's Early Work on Capability to Choice and sustainability'. Personal correspondence.

Klein, N. (2001), *No Logo*. London: Flamingo.

Kotter, J. P. (199), *Leading Change*. Boston: Harvard Business School Press.

Laurillard, D. (1993). *Rethinking University Teaching: A Framework for the Effective Use of Educational Technology*. Routledge, London.

Layard, R. (2005), *Happiness*. London: Penguin.

Leadbeater, C. (2000), *Living on Thin Air: The New Economy*. London: Penguin.

Leadbetter, C. (2004), *Learning about Personalisation*. London: Demos.

Levin, B. (2001), *Reforming Education: From Origins to Outcomes*. London: Routledge Falmer.

Lindström, M., and Seybold, P. (2003), *Brandchild: Remarkable Insights into the Minds of Today's Global Kids and their Relationships with Brands*. London: Kogan Page.

Laming, W. H. (2003), *The Victoria Climbié Inquiry*. Norwich: Her Majesty's Stationery Office.

Machado, A. (1978), *Caminante, son tus huellas*. (trans. Betty Jeane Craige). Louisiana: Louisiana State University.

Monbiot, G. (2001), *Captive State: The Corporate Takeover of Britain*. London: Pan.

Nietzche, F. (2005), *Thus Spoke Zarathustra*. (trans. Graham Parkes). Oxford: Oxford University Press.

Nolan, R. L. (2000), 'Information Technology Management since 1960' In A. D. Chandler and J. W. Cortoda (eds), *A Nation Transformed by Information: How Information has shaped the United States from Colonial Times to the Present*. Oxford: Oxford University Press, 271–56.

Nolan, R. L. and Croson, D. C. (1995), *Creative Destruction: A Six-Stage Process for Transforming the Organization*. Boston: Harvard Business School Press.

Oblinger, D. and Oblinger, J. (eds) (2005), *Educating the Net Generation*. Washington: Educause.

Ormerod, P. (2005), *Why Most Things Fail: Evolution, Exstinction and Economics*. Hoboken: John Wiley and Sons.

Orr, D. (1994), *Earth in Mind*. New York: First Island Press.

O'Sullivan, E. (1999), *Transformative Learning: Educational Vision for the 21st Century*. London: Zed Books.

Orwell, G. (1949), *1984*. London: Secker and Warburg.

Overy, R. (2009*)*, *The Morbid Age*. London: Allen Lane.

Pea, R.D. (1993), 'Practices of Distributed Intelligence and Designs for Education' in Salomon, G. (ed.) *Distributed Cognitions*. Cambridge: Cambridge University Press.

Perkins, D. (1992), *Smart Schools*. New York: The Free Press

Pinker, S. (2003), *The Blank Slate*. London: Penguin.

Porritt, J. (2009), 'Living within our Means: Avoiding the Ultimate Recession'. London: Forum for the Future.

Postman, N. (1996), *The End of Education*. New York: Knopf.

Prensky, M. (2002), *What Kids Learn That's POSITIVE From Playing Video Games*. www.marcprensky.com/writing. Accessed 18 May 2008.

PricewaterhouseCoopers (2001), *Teacher Workload Study: Final Report*. London: DfES Publications.

PricewaterhouseCoopers (2007), *Independent Study into School Leadership*. Nottingham: DfES Publications.

Putnam, R. D. (2000), *Bowling Alone: The Collapse and Revival of American Community*. New York: Simon and Schuster.

Reimer, E. (1971), *School is Dead. An Essay on Alternatives in Education*. Harmondsworth: Penguin.

Ridley, M. (2003), *Nature via Nurture*. London: HarperCollins.

Rousseau, J-J. (1974), *Emile*. (trans. B. Foxley). London: J. M. Dent.

Sachs, W. (1992), *The Development Dictionary: A Guide to Knowledge as Power*. London: Zed Books.

Schwartz, D. (1997), *Who Cares? Rediscovering Community*. Boulder: Westview.

Seely Brown, J. and Duguid, P. (2001), *The Social Life of Information: Learning in the Digital Age*. Boston: Harvard Business School Press.

Sen, A. (1999), *Development as Freedom*. Oxford: Oxford Books.

Siemens, G. (2006), *Knowing Knowledge*. Canada: Complexive Inc.

Silins, H. and Mulford, B. (2002), 'Leadership and School Results' in Leithwood, K. and Hallinger, P. (eds) *Second International Handbook of Educational Leadership and Administration*. Norwell: Kluwer Academic Press.

Smith, A. (1976), *An Inquiry into the Nature and Causes of the Wealth of Nations*, vol. 1. Chicago: University of Chicago Press.

Smith, A. (2004), *The Brain's Behind It*. Stafford: Network Educational Press.

Smith, L. G. and Smith, J. K. (1994), *Lives in Education*. New York: St Martin's Press.

Smithers, A. and Robinson, P. (2008), *HMC Schools: A Quantitative Analysis* Buckingham: Buckingham Centre for Education and Employment Research, University of Buckingham.

Soros, G. (2008), *The New Paradigm for Financial Markets*. New York: Public Affairs Books.

Spillane, J. P. (2006), *Distributed Leadership*. San Francisco: Jossey-Bass.

Steeples, C. and Jones, C. (eds) (2002), *Networked Learning: Perspectives and Issues*. Berlin: Springer-Verlag.

Steffen, A. www.worldchanging.com/. Sourced 11 November 2008.

Stefkovich, J. and Begley, P. (2007), 'Ethical School Leadership: Defining the Best Interests of Students', *Educational Management Administration and Leadership,* vol. 35, no. 2, 205–24.

Stephenson, J., Ling, L., Burman, E., and Cooper ,M. (1998), *Values in Education*. Abingdon: Routledge.

Sternberg, R. J. (1990), *Metaphors of Mind*. Cambridge: Cambridge University Press.

Surowiecki, J. (2004), *The Wisdom of Crowds: Why the Many Are Smarter Than the Few and How Collective Wisdom Shapes Business, Economies, Societies and Nations*. London: Little, Brown.

Taleb, N. (2008), *The Black Swan: The Impact of the Highly Improbable*. London: Penguin.

Tapscott, D. (1998), *Growing up Digital: The Rise of the Net Generation*. New York: McGraw-Hill.

TDA, *Remodelling Change Process*. www.tda.gov.uk/remodelling/managingchange/remodellingprocess.

TDA (2007a), *Professional Standards for Teachers: Why Sit Still in your Career?* London: TDA Publications.

TDA (2007b), *Higher Level Teaching Assistant: Candidate Handbook*. London: TDA Publications.

TDA (2007c), *The National Occupational Standards (NOS) for Supporting Teaching and Learning in Schools*. www.tda.gov.uk/leaders/supportstaff/NOS/Supporting_teaching_learning.aspx.

TDA (2008a), *School Improvement Planning Framework*. www.tda.gov.uk/about/publicationslisting/TDA0570.aspx.

TDA (2008b), *Parent Support Adviser Toolkit v2*. http://www.tda.gov.uk/about/publicationslisting/TDA0514.aspx.

Teaching and Learning Research Council (2007), *Neuroscience and Education: Issues and Opportunities*. TLRP.

The Times,(2005), *'Schools to Encourage Emotional Intelligence'*. (28 November 2005).

Toffler, A. (1970), *Future Shock*. London: Bodley Head.

Toffler, A. and Toffler, H. (2006), *Revolutionary Wealth*. New York: Knopf Publishers.

Van der Zanden, A. H. W. (2009), *The Facilitating University: Positioning the Next Generation Higher Education* (forthcoming). Delft: TU Delft.

Van der Zanden, A. H. W. and Veen, W. (2004), 'Hypothetical Model for Change and Progress of ICT in Education' in: Yasser, A., Smit, R. and Halil, T. (eds), *New Directions in Technology Management: Changing Collaboration Between Government, Industry and University* IAMOT. (TUD), 1–15.

Veen, W.,and Jacobs, F. (2005), *Leren van Jongeren: Een Literatuuronderzoek naar Nieuwe Geletterdheid*. Utrecht: Stichting SURF.

Veen, W. and Vrakking, B. (2006), *Homo Zappiens: Growing Up in a Digital Age*. London: Network Continuum Education.

Vygotsky, L. S. (1978), *Mind in Society*. Cambridge: Harvard University Press.

Warnock Report: Special Educational Needs (1978) London: HMSO.

Wells, H. G. (1923), *Men Like Gods*. London: Cassell.

Wenger, E. (1998), *Communities of Practice: Learning, Meaning and Identity*. Cambridge: Cambridge University Press.

West-Burnham, J. and Coates, M. (2005) *Personalizing Learning, Transforming Education for Every Child*. London: Network Educational Press.

Whitehead, A. (2008), *How Emotional Intelligence Affects Behaviour*. www.teachingexpertise.com/articles/how-emotional-intelligence-affects-behaviour-1438.

www.webtitanic.net. Accessed 29 September 2009.

Index

Hallinger, P.   76
Halstead, Mark, *Values in Education and Education in Values*   26
Handy, Charles   24
Harker, Lisa   135
Harris, Alma   70–6
Hauerwas, Stanley   29–30, 31–2
Havel, Václav   5
headteachers
    of independent schools   98, 100, 102
    and leadership   72, 73, 92–3
health and well-being in schools   37
Heifetz, Ron   71
higher education, and change teams in schools   47
Hitler, Adolf   27
HLTAs (Higher Level Teaching Assistants)   35, 39, 44, 46, 47
Hobsbawm, E.   79
Hock, Dee   5–6
Holmes, Brian   89
Homo Zappiens   121–4, 127
Hopkins, David   61–9, 73
human capital   78, 81, 82
Hurstpierpoint College   99–100
Hutchings, Edward, *Cognition in the Wild*   72

ICT (information and communication technology)   13, 58, 87, 121–7
    future of   128–9
Illich, Ivan   79
independence   14, 15
independent schools   95–103
    and community outreach   100–2
    government policies on   101–2
    and personalization   96–8
    values   98–9
Independent State School Partnerships grant scheme   101
Independent Study into School Leadership (PricewaterhouseCoopers)   38
individual learning   58
individuals, and independent schools   96–8
Industrial Revolution   19, 20
inequalities   14, 111
    educational achievement   37
    university admissions   23
Innovation Unit   135
    Communities for Learning initiative   46
institutional factors, in education issues   88, 89
Integrated Qualification Framework (IQF)   37, 42

intelligence
    emotional   53–4, 117–18
    and learning   55–6
    multiple intelligences   117–18
interagency working   42
interdependence   14, 15, 112
    and community   81–2
International Monetary Fund   21
internet   121, 124, 128
    social networking sites   82, 129
interpersonal intelligence   117
intrapersonal intelligence   117
IQ   54, 55–6, 134
IQF (Integrated Qualification Framework)   37, 42

James, Chris   94
Joyce, B.   48
Juba Diocesan Model Secondary School (Sudan)   137
Jung, Carl   107

Kaufmann, Dr Liane   108
Kay, Alan   16
Keynesian economics   21
King's Hall preparatory school   99
Kolb's Experiential Learning Model   109
Kotter, John, principles of change   40

Laming equiry   43
Lancing College   100, 101
language learning   16
Leadbetter, C.   51, 80
leadership
    current structures of   71
    distributed   72–4, 75, 76
    future challenges   70–6
    global context of school leadership   85–94
    and learning   60
    roles in schools   35, 36
    system-wide school transformation   6, 61, 62, 64–5, 65, 66
leading schools   66, 68
learning   51–60
    and communities   57, 77–8
    formal education and personal learning   114–20
    future of   59
    and intelligence   55–6
    leadership and the learning environment   74–5